The "Black" and "White" of Racism

The "Black" and "White" of Racism

A COMMENTARY
FROM A DIFFERENT PERSPECTIVE
ABOUT RACE RELATIONS
AND REASON FOR ALARM

. . .

Waylon Allen

First Edition

ISBN: 1542598893
ISBN 13: 9781542598897

Introduction

. . .

Did you know that the first official slave owner in Colonial America was a "Black" African?

Did you know that there were many "Black" slave owners in early America up until the time of the Civil War?

Did you know that there were many "White" slaves that came from Europe?

Did you know that Slavery still exists today in some countries?

These are some of the surprising facts the author discovered while researching racism and race relations in early America through today.

When his teenage granddaughter mentioned that she did not like a group of people with a certain skin color, the author decided to respond to her with a letter against racism. After looking deeper into the subject, he realized that the true facts and the current perception of the facts were different. He came to feel that he had been misinformed over the years and misled by the general consensus regarding what actually occurred from the time of the initial settling of the Colonies until the Civil War regarding slavery. The letter evolved into this "Commentary" regarding racism and race relations.

He came to the conclusion that we, as a Nation, cannot resolve our racial divisions until the real truth is known and realized by all American citizens. He states that, *"Hidden in the actual truth is the resolution for the animosity and resentment that separates us as a united people"*.

The author provides informative insight into how racism is maintained in a manner that affects almost all American citizens today and how we can join together to resolve what he calls this *"racialist affliction"* that grips our Nation.

Reasons for alarm are cited and solutions are suggested in this challenging but refreshing commentary about the very difficult issue of racism and race relations in America. -- Ray Bennett

Dedicated
To
All
Full
Blooded
American
Citizens

Subjects

"Facts do not cease to exist because they are ignored (I)... And ye shall know the truth, and the truth shall set you free (II)...a house divided against itself will not stand (III)... America! America! And crown thy good with brotherhood from sea to shining sea!" (IV)

(I)   Aldous Huxley
(II)   John 8:32 KJV
(III) Matthew 12:25 KJV
(IV) America the Beautiful, words by Katharine Lee Bates

Why This Was Written

. . .

While taking my granddaughter to a doctor's appointment she told me that she does not like white people. She went on to say that she feels most white people are racists and treat black people badly. She also said that many police officers are racists and "bad cops".

I was a bit shocked and confused. My granddaughter is 17 years old, of Scottish and Italian heritage, comes from a liberal household that strongly supported Barack Obama for President. Her only experience with a police officer is when one stopped to help her when her car was stalled in traffic.

I did not know what to say and wondered if she included me and her family as white people she does not like. I let it pass and changed the subject. However, the brief conversation continued to be of concern to me and, I felt, needed a response.

So here goes. I am directing this response to her, but wish to offer it for consideration by other people who might be interested in the subject of racism.

Dear Nicole,

Your recent comments about you not liking "white people" and "bad cops" were troubling to me and, I feel, deserve a considered response.

Since you were very explicit in stating that you do not like people who are "white", I have to assume that you do not dislike people in general, but specifically people you consider classified as "White".

My first reaction, when considering your statement, was to question how you came to have such negative feelings about people you consider "white", and what made you think they are racist.

Then I remembered that your very close friend is of African heritage. I have to wonder if your feelings are being influenced by your relationship with her.

Regardless, to address your statement, I have to deal with the varied implications that your statement suggest. It seems to me that your issue is with race and race relations.

Your statement that you do not like "White" people is indicative of the racial antagonism that is so pervasive in America today. At times the animosity reaches the level of hate. It is not a person not liking another person for some reason. It is a person, like yourself, not liking other people in generalized broad categories based on perceptions of race determined by skin pigmentation.

It is perhaps the most volatile and divisive issue we face in our nation today. It is also the most perilous internal threat America has ever had to deal with. Our country is literally unraveling with racial polarization into a form of tribalism that can only lead to increasing civil disorder.

For this reason, I am going to deal with this issue of race and race relations in a frank and open manner. I am also going to address my comments to the general public as well. My hope is to help start a national open discussion regarding racism and race relations. Understand that the formality of my comments are because I am speaking to all the citizens in our nation as well as yourself.

I understand that this document will perhaps be somewhat challenging to read. I am trying to be precise in language to express my thoughts and suppositions. In addition, I have attempted to provide factually verifiable information with detailed supporting references.

I assure you that your effort to read the material will be rewarded with expanded informational insight into the issues relating to racism, and may well contribute to your being able to participate in making improvements to race relations in our nation.

Of course this is an extremely contentious subject. I understand that in these times of political correctness and stifled free speech, my comments herewith will draw adverse criticism from some, perhaps many. This will serve to obtain my objective.

We need to have an open candid discussion from individuals on all sides and points of view. Hopefully, we can discuss the reality associated with the issues, not emotional reactions, in a civil and constructive discourse.

As individuals, and as a nation, we need to acknowledge the critical nature of the situation and start talking with each other as concerned citizens of this wonderful nation seeking to resolve our racial divisions

Following, Nicole, is the response that your statement prompted.

WORDS

Nicole, remember recently when I suggested that you increase your vocabulary as much as possible because your mind uses words in the thinking process and that words can expand your intellectual ability?

Much of this writing is about words and how their meaning effects our minds.

I have read that there are about 220,000 words in the Oxford English dictionary. Merriam Webster notes that *"It has been estimated that the vocabulary of English includes roughly 1 million words..."* (1)

These words in essence symbolize the entire knowledge we have as English speaking human beings when arranged into thoughts and expressions. Words then cause a mental process that makes us intelligent, and to some degree, our individual intelligence is associated with our understanding the meaning of words.

So to understand the above statement, *that words symbolize knowledge*, we need to understand what "symbolize" means. The word "symbolize" represents something other than the word itself. This is what a symbol is. It conveys a meaning, but only if another person knows and understands the assigned meaning.

For example you can say an English word to someone who speaks another language and that word will have no meaning to them. In the same way if a person speaking English, does not understand the meaning of a particular English word, then naturally, the word has no meaning to them.

So words are useless without meaning and the general understanding of that meaning. This is the reason I urge you to use your dictionary when you are not sure of a word.

I also urge you to research some of the statements in this writing which you might question to either confirm or disprove my accuracy. I do not expect you to accept what I say here without question. I truly want you to find out for yourself if my facts, suppositions and assumptions are reasonable and valid.

You will notice that I will be using words such as "racialism", "racialist", and "racialistic" in addition to the word "racism". The dictionary relates these words to the original French "racisme" which became racism with the definition implying racial superiority and inferiority to some groups.

I am using the other words associated with racism to denote an attitude whereby a person assigns racial categories in grouping people based on skin pigmentation ranging in hue from light to dark. This "racialistic" attitude also assigns stereotypical attributes, imposed on individuals, that are generalized based on perceived racial purity. These "racialists" are, in varying degrees, obsessed with racial designations rather than individual distinctions.

Words Can Be Ambiguous

Unfortunately, words can also be used to mislead or even deceive the thinking process. While the words "White People" provides a quick thought concept that describes a particular grouping of people and separates them from "Black People", for example, the meaning of the words can be modified to infuse the thought process with false and erroneous meaning and understanding.

For you, the meaning you have associated with the words "White People" has embedded in your brain a mental concept that is triggered anytime to see, mention or think about a light skinned individual. Your mind immediately projects your negative mental concept toward that person even if that "white" person had just arrived from Africa where they spent years helping the "black people" overcome AIDS. Your brain is infected with Racialism because of the connotation you have associated with the words "White People" even though, actually, there is no such thing as a "White Person or White People".

Anthropologists suggest that there are four major race classifications with about 30 subgroups here on Earth. The major races are designated as Caucasoid, Negroid, Mongoloid and Australoid.

While I do not subscribe to this classification of humans, if you want to be more accurate scientifically and academically in your racial classification, it would be better to use these words in your thinking process.

However, the fact is that all races share over 99% of the same genetic material. We all belong to the same species, which is Homo sapiens. And most of us are, to some degree, of mixed race. You cannot tell by skin color. Only a DNA test could give an accurate description of the racial mix. Some of us even have the remnants of Neanderthals from long, long ago. Yet none of this says very much about the individual person. You cannot classify, describe or summarize accurately an individual human with a term like "White" or "Caucasian".

A college class at West Chester University in Pennsylvania used DNA testing of saliva to show how "mixed up" we Americans actually are racially. In a Washington Post online article by Susan Syrluga which was published December 24, 2016 with the headline suggesting, "To bring a divided country together, start with a little split". Instructor Anita Foeman asked her students to take the DNA test with interesting results. The article notes:

"Instead of a confrontational approach, trying to provoke people into recognizing their own biases, (Anita Foeman) wanted something that would pull people together, or at least give them a neutral place from which to start to talk. And with racial divides so stark, she wanted to add some nuance and depth. She wondered: What if people started finding out things they didn't know about themselves?"

The results demonstrated the racial mix:

"...When I opened my results, the first thing that greeted me was 6 percent African," said a student with light skin in the back of the classroom, smacking herself in the forehead, mouth open wide, to recreate her reaction the night before: 'Whaaaaat?'

'I guess I shouldn't be that surprised,' she added. 'I know a lot of African American people have some white DNA, so I shouldn't be surprised there's some African in me'.

...One woman of Chinese descent told Foeman, 'It's okay for you — you already know you're mixed up. I don't want to find out I'm not pure'.

...Foeman has seen people drop out of the project after getting their results, including three people who identified as African American who were upset to find out how much European ancestry they had. Some people refuse to take the test.

...The DNA test 'helps us understand we're not all from one special place, which is really peculiar to America,' Foeman said. 'Because we're all from different areas, with different ideas that come with that ethnic culture. What makes America great is we have all those cultures combined'.

...Foeman, who is African American — and genetically more than one-quarter European, as she now knows — would like to test as many people as she can. ... Most of all, she'd like to get everyone talking." (2)

You can use the word "White", you can think the word, but you cannot rely on the accuracy or validity of the word in reference to people. A bed sheet can be white, but an individual human cannot be, and should not be, defined as white. It does not even accurately depict the individual's skin tone unless the person is perhaps an albino.

I am reminded of a statement made by Martin Luther King:

"I have a dream that my four little children will one day live in a nation where they will not be judged by the colour of their skin but by the content of their character".

Nicole, are you, in fact, making judgements and assigning dislike based solely on skin color?

USING WORDS TO MISLEAD AND CONFUSE

Politicians often misuse words to fool the people. You likely have heard of what is called "Obama Care". Critics of the legislation used this term rather than the name of the legislation because they felt it would fail and wanted the failure associated with President Obama.

Conversely, the Obama administration called it the "Affordable Care Act" to imply that the legislation would make health care more affordable for most people. The deception was in the word "Affordable". It was used purposely to deceive.

Jonathan Gruber, a professor of economics at MIT, who helped name the bill and was one of the architects of the legislation, has been shown on a video mocking *"the stupidity"* of the American voter for not perceiving the ways in which the controversial health law concealed its true cost.

> *"(Gruber) sparked a furor after video surfaced of his talking about the 'stupidity' of the American people, among other insults aimed at the voting public."* (3)
>
> *(To view the Video go to YouTube and search "Too Stupid to Understand". Actually you will find three videos there with Gruber calling the American people "Stupid")*

A CBS New York online article noted the actual increasing cost of the "Affordable" health care plan:

> *"The Department of Health and Human Services revealed Monday that premiums for a midlevel benchmark plan will increase by the average of 25 percent across the 39 states served by the federally run online market. ...However, in Arizona, unsubsidized premiums for a hypothetical 27-year*

*old buying a benchmark 'second-lowest cost 'Silver' plan
will jump by 116 percent, from $196 to $422, according to
the administration report"* (4)

So to use the official name of the federal health plan, we have
to use the word "Affordable" while obviously it is rising to
"Unaffordable" levels. Another aspect of this deceit was that
the cost increases were hidden and delayed until sometime after
the bill was implemented.

In fact, there is a word for people who misinform through
the use of words and spread misinformation and rumors to manipulate and confuse the public. The word is "Propagandist" and
they disseminate "propaganda" not to inform but to confound
the truth.

We must be careful how words can be used to influence our
minds and thinking at the same time we are using words for clari-
fication and understanding. We can fool ourselves with words
and we can be fooled using words by others.

DEFINING PEOPLE BY COLOR GROUPS

Let me begin by stating that, very often, when someone describes people by color and accuse someone else of racism, then that someone most often has a racialistic mind-set themselves. They might deny it, but their words reveal how their mind functions.

For example, to me, you talk like a racialist and seem to have the mental process of a racist. A statement like "I do not like white people" is a strong indication of how you think. It meets the definition of racism which is "hatred or intolerance of another race or racial group". In addition, being a racialist can describe a person that sees individual people by race classification while holding preconceived notions regarding the various races.

You think using racial and racist terms like "white or black" which has programed your mind to think as a racialist. When you see an individual your mind immediately categorizes that person by color with all the racial bias you have accumulated in association with that word. It is like a mental infection that channels your thinking through a racial lens. For this reason a racialist is unable to see the individual person impartially and without prejudice.

A person without a racialistic mind-set will initially see only a human being. They will then begin to form opinions about that person based on the mental and physical actions of that person. They begin by knowing nothing about the person they have just met without projecting any presuppositions toward that person. They will then make determinations regarding that person based solely on their personal experience with that person.

You are not alone, however, in assigning racial generalities based on perceived skin color grouping. Actually, many, perhaps most, people are likewise programed in a similar manner without actually being aware. Our government and educational institutions perpetuate this racial condition of mind by continuing to categorize individual citizens with terms like "White" or "Black".

Race designation using "White", "Black", "Brown" and whatever else is in the racial color spectrum, divides us and polarizes us against each other as individual citizens. This makes it absolutely impossible for us to get along as individual citizens. It is making harmony among individual American citizens impossible and contributes to an increasing sense of tribalism and divided "communities" in this nation.

This in turn is contributing to growing racial hostility and racial strife. Unless we change the course, we face serious impending race based civil conflict.

TIME TO MOVE BEYOND RACE

First, as I stated prior, there is no such group as "White People" or "Black People". You are stereotyping a very diverse and very dissimilar group of people into a racial classification because their skin happens to be somewhat similar in tone. If you were to assemble a thousand so called "White People" or "Black People" and check out their life experience, education, beliefs, attitudes and DNA, as a racialist, you would be amazed at the vast individual differences. I feel you would intellectually have to abandon your assertion that "White People" or "Black People" can be grouped, stereotyped and described by such a simplistic term as "White" or "Black". I further feel sure you could not justify your dislike for such a wide range grouping of individual people perceived to have "light skin color" by using the word "White".

I suspect that, as a racialist, you consider President Obama as being "Black". For example, while President Obama has a skin tone you would not consider "White", he is perhaps more a "White Person" than a "Black Person". He developed from an embryo for nine months in the body of a light skinned "White" woman. He was nourished in his development in the womb by a "White" woman's placenta and pushed and pulled from her "White" body into the World. He was raised and grew up in the household of his "White" grandparents. If you could check his DNA you would be convinced that he can qualify as being a "White" as well as a "Black" person using your racial classification.

I must say that I regret that, as president, he did not make the point that he transcends race and is simply an individual American citizen. Once again racialism won out and the polarization of our nation into race and racism was strengthened by him defining himself using the racialistic words "Black Person".

AM I A "RED" MAN?

You may not be aware that some of my ancestry is Native pre-American. My father was what people call an "Indian". Despite his heritage and the atrocities some of my family said was perpetrated on the native peoples, my dad loved America and what he felt was the wonderful civilization that was brought to this continent. He understood and agreed that the native peoples were abused and brutally mistreated, as well as culturally annihilated, but he also felt that dwelling on the loss and change was useless and even more destructive for the future of people like himself.

While my dad disliked talking about my "native" heritage, my uncles often told me about the "Shawnee" ways and the "proud" history of our "tribal clan" much to my dad's disdain.

I was told that a fellow named Tecumseh was a dead hero relative and was much revered by my uncle named "William Tecumseh". He told me that "our people" had struggled fiercely against the "European Invaders" with Tecumseh trying vainly to unite the native tribes to fight together. He said that "tribal differences" caused Tecumseh to fail.

I was torn between my dad's disinterest in his "Indian" heritage and my uncle's pride in his ancestry and resentment of the American people who, he felt, had destroyed their culture and way of life.

Then as a very young child, my mother's sister took me to my first "Cowboys and Indians" movie. I left devastated and in shock. When I got home I asked my dad if he and my uncle were "Savages". He told me "no" and that we were quite "civilized". He said he was a "printer" by trade and enjoyed living in the city.

I then asked him if I was a "half breed". I knew my mother was of German ancestry.

He then set me down at the kitchen table and became very serious. He said, "Son, you are a full blooded American Citizen. You live in a country where most people are mixed. There are no pure bloods in this country."

This is when he told me something that, in essence, caused me to completely lose interest in understanding what being an "Indian" had meant and to realize what being an American Citizen means to me.

He said that, as an American, I have very personal and "Individual" rights as a citizen. He said that the United States Constitution and Bill of Rights assured me of my "individual rights" and protected me as an individual from the government and even the majority, should they attempt to take them away from me. He said that the Constitution and Bill of Rights cited "God" as the ultimate authority and that no one can take these rights from me as an individual as long as America survived as a nation.

He told me that George Washington was the best "Chief" a people could have had and that our way of life as "American Citizens" was far superior to what our life would have been within an Indian tribe.

I have been a proud "Full Blooded American" ever since.

I must admit that I resent being called, referred to, or designated as a "White" or "Red" person. It is an insult to a "Full Blooded American Citizen".

RACIALISM HAS BEEN INSTITUTIONALIZED

Unfortunately, as I stated before, this dividing of the citizens of America is supported by the government, as well as, educational institutions and the majority of people in America. I see all types of forms that ask me to designate my race. There are often check boxes with such words as "White", "Black", "Hispanic", "Native American", and "Alaskan Native". To use these words to classify people is not only simplistic and incorrect, but is also overtly racialistic.

These lists force a person to subliminally incorporate the racist connotation into their vocabulary and thinking. What is missing, from my point of view, is the designation of "Mixed", "Not Sure" or "Ambiguous". Or better yet "Full Blooded American Citizen". Wouldn't it be wonderful if most people listed the latter?

Even though it is known that the DNA of most citizens are racially mixed and varied, racialistic minded people perpetuate the myth that skin tone can be used to divide people into cohesive racial groups that are facsimiles of each other. Professors in our Universities, pride themselves at being intelligent individuals while under the influence of a racialistic mind-set. They participate in projecting the classification of "race" on other people while they pretend to take some intellectual high ground racially. They even allow and support the students who polarize into these pseudo racial groups. I seldom hear or read about educators attempting to dispel the myth of "pure race" and "stereotyped individual life experiences". These racialistic educators personify the full meaning of the word "ignorant" in this regard.

For politicians, the race division works to herd and manipulate individual citizens into thinking that they are better served, as a racial group, by one political party or another.

As alluded to prior, if you were to check the demographics of all the individual people in America, you would find that the economic, educational, life experience, and total racial heritage of each individual is varied and different. Likely you would not find any two individuals, outside each person's family, that are just alike regardless of skin color and tone.

You would find that there are very rich people both so called "White" and "Black". You would also find that there are very poor people of all skin colors. Being a particular skin color does not exclude that individual from being wealthy or less fortunate economically.

Regardless of what you may think or have been told, if an individual can excel in this nation, then they will likely prosper.

You do not see many so called "White" professional basketball players. This is not because "white" basketball players are discriminated against, or are unable to play the game. The reason so called "Black" people dominate the field is because they each individually excel at the sport. There are some sports that so called "White" players seem to excel. In each individual case, the achievement in the sport is based on individual ability and personal drive. This achievement through individual excellence is reflected throughout all aspects of sports, business, science and entertainment in America.

The fact is that there are more poor and uneducated so called "White" people in America today than poor and uneducated so called "Black" people. This fact is an indication that skin color and tone alone does not assure prosperity or poverty. It is a racialistic over simplification that puts forth the myth that achievement is obtained or restrained by skin color alone.

Sometimes, however, a racialistic mind-set and attitude can limit a person's efforts to achieve. More often it's a person's efforts and determination that most influences that person's accomplishments.

Had my dad remained on the Indian reservation and seethed in resentment for events of the past, then he too would surely have failed to become a fully enfranchised American Citizen. His decision, then, might have limited the accomplishments of his children who might have remained on the reservation as well. One generation can absolutely influence the accomplishments and future of the next. This way a racialist can bequeath to their children a path toward failure.

Only by abandoning and overcoming racialism can a person hope to obtain the full benefits of being a citizen in the land of individual freedom and opportunity. A racialist is not truly free and opportunity is easily lost. It is not skin color that holds an individual back in America. It is often ability, expectation, attitude and determination that overcomes disadvantage.

We have dark skinned people immigrating to this country from India. Many come from circumstances that an average American would consider very poor economically. Often their skin is as dark as many so called "Blacks". Yet they excel in fields of technology, science and medicine. As in the field of Basketball, the most capable and qualified excel and achieve in their perspective fields. For a racialist that uses skin tone and color as a racial designation there might be a dilemma here. They might want to think of successful immigrants from India in terms of very dark skinned "White" people just to make everything fit in the racialist mind-set.

The Word "Slavery"

I suspect that this word has some influence on your attitude regarding what you call "White People".

What comes to your mind when you think this word? Is it associated specifically with "white" people enslaving "black" people? If so, once again, a word associated with false information has deluded your mind with a racialist myth.

To enlighten your mind regarding this word consider these facts and do some research to verify the validity of these facts.

"One of the most vexing questions in African-American history is whether free African Americans themselves owned slaves. The short answer to this question, as you might suspect, is yes, of course; some free black people in this country bought and sold other black people, and did so at least since 1654, continuing to do so right through the Civil War." (5)

"In a fascinating essay reviewing this controversy, R. Halliburton shows that free black people have owned slaves "in each of the thirteen original states and later in every state that countenanced slavery," at least since Anthony Johnson and his wife Mary went to court in Virginia in 1654 to obtain the services of their indentured servant, a black man, John Castor, for life.

And for a time, free black people could even "own" the services of white indentured servants in Virginia as well. Free blacks owned slaves in Boston by 1724 and in Connecticut by 1783; by 1790, 48 black people in Maryland owned 143 slaves. One particularly notorious black

Maryland farmer named Nat Butler "regularly purchased and sold Negroes for the Southern trade," Halliburton wrote." (6)

Another misconception is that a majority of the people in the South, prior to the Civil War, owned African slaves. I did a calculation from the 1860 census. (7)

Overall in the Nation with a population of 31,183,582 "Free Citizens", 393,975 individuals were listed as "Slave Holders". Therefore 1% of the Nation's citizens owned slaves in 1860.

In the 13 states making up the Southern Confederacy, there was a population of 5,582,222 "Free Citizens" with 316,632 individuals listed as "Slave Holders". Therefore 6% of the Confederate States citizens owned slaves in 1860

There is, however, some confusion regarding these numbers because some researchers figure the percentage of "Southern Families" that owned slaves. This percentage is closer to 39.7 % if using slave holders' families. Since individuals, not families owned slaves, using the percent per family is not factually correct. This is indicating that even the wives and children of the families owned the slaves which is not the case. Admittedly, however, the families benefited from the slave labor and were subject to inheriting the slaves at the death of the owner.

But even using the family numbers, the fact is that about 60% of the families in the South, in 1860, did not own slaves.

"As for free Negroes in the southern states, about 10% owned slaves". (8)

A more accurate depiction of life in the South prior to the Civil War states:

> *"Most people and families in the South led a pastoral life, organized around agricultural activities. Most families had either no slaves or very few, so the men and children did the physical labor."* (9)

"WHITE" SLAVES

It is even more erroneous to associate enslaved people with primarily "black people". In fact, so called "White" people suffered enslavement throughout history. Consider and verify these facts from the book, *"They Were White and They Were Slaves, The Untold History of the Enslavement of Whites in Early America"*, by Michael A. Hoffman II. The book has excellent documentation of the facts presented. I encourage you to read this very thorough history of Caucasian slavery for further edification.

> *"This is a history of White people that has never been told in any coherent form, largely because most modern historians have, for reasons of politics or psychology, refused to recognize White slaves in early America as just that. Today, not a tear is shed for the sufferings of millions of our own enslaved forefathers. 200 years of White slavery in America have been almost completely obliterated from the collective memory of the American people.*

The author quotes from an article in the Las Angeles Times:

> *'Who wants to be reminded that half--perhaps as many as two-thirds--of the original American colonists came here, not of their own free will, but kidnapped, shanghaied, impressed, duped, beguiled, and yes, in chains?... we tend to gloss over it... we'd prefer to forget the whole sorry chapter...'(Elaine Kendall, Los Angeles Times, Sept. 1, 1985).*

The author further notes:

A correct understanding of the authentic history of the enslavement of Whites in America could have profound consequences for the future of the races.

'We cannot be sure that the position of the earliest Africans differed markedly from that of the white indentured servants. The debate has considerable significance for the interpretation of race relations in American history.

The author points out the failure of educators and media to tell the full truth about Caucasian slavery:

It is interesting that White people who were bound to a condition of what became in many cases permanent chattel slavery unto death, are not referred to as slaves by Establishment academics. With the massive concentration of educational and media resources on the negro experience of slavery the unspoken assumption has been that only Blacks have been enslaved to any degree or magnitude worthy of study or memorial. The historical record reveals that this is not the case, however. White people have been sold as slaves for centuries." (10)

If you have an opportunity to visit Mount Vernon, George Washington's plantation in Alexandria Virginia, you will find that there were slave housing for both "White" and "Black" slaves.

Should you research further the history of slavery, you will find that slavery has a deplorable human history that includes Caucasoid, Negroid and most of the races of humanity, likely going back as far as recorded human history.

THE "FOUNDING FATHER" OF SLAVERY IN COLONIAL AMERICA

I wonder if most people realize that the first official slave owner in the American colonies was an African.

"The first official slave owner in America was an Angolan who adopted the European name of Anthony Johnson. He was sold to the slave traders in 1621 by an enemy tribe in his native Africa, and was registered as "Antonio, a Negro: in the official records of the Colony of Virginia.

Prior to 1654, all Africans in the thirteen colonies were held in indentured servitude and were released after a contracted period with many of the indentured receiving land and equipment after their contracts for work expired. Johnson would later take ownership of a large plot of farmland after the expiration of his contract and, using the skills he had learned during his indentured labor service, Johnson became moderately successful.

By July 1651, Johnson had five indentured servants of his own. In 1664, he brought a case before Virginia courts in which he contested a suit launched by one of his indentured servants, a Negro who adopted the name John Casor. Johnson won the suit and retained Casor as his servant for life, who thus became the first official and true slave in America." (11)

"BLACK" SLAVE OWNERS

Of course, while Anthony Johnson was one of the first African slaveholders, there were many more who owned slaves up to the time of the Civil War.

"Many free Negros owned black slaves, in fact, in numbers disproportionate to their representation in society at large.

In 1830, a fourth of the free Negro slave masters in South Carolina owned 10 or more slaves; eight owning 30 or more.

According to federal census reports, on June 1, 1860 there were nearly 4.5 million Negros in the United States, with fewer than four million of them living in the southern slaveholding states.

Of the blacks residing in the South, 261,988 were not slaves. Of this number, 10,689 lived in New Orleans, Duke University professor John Hope Franklin, of African heritage, recorded that in New Orleans over 3,000 free Negros owned slaves, or 28 percent of the free Negros in that city.

In 1860 there were at least six Negroes in Louisiana who owned 65 or more slaves. The largest number, 152 slaves, were owned by the widow C. Richards and her son P.C. Richards, who owned a large sugar cane plantation.

Another Negro slave magnate in Louisiana with over 100 slaves was Antoine Dubuclet, a sugar planter whose estate was values at (in 1860 dollars) $264,000.

In Charleston, South Carolina in 1860 125 free Negros owned slaves, six of them owning 10 or more. Of the $1.5 *million in taxable property owned by free Negroes in Charleston, more than $300,000 represented slave holdings. In North Carolina 69 free Negros were slave owners"* (12)

I came across this brief biography item in an old history textbook while researching. It gives a close up look at a successful "Black" slaveholder in the period:

"John Carruthers Stanley of New Bern (North Carolina) was the largest black slaveholder in the entire South. Stanly was a barber who received his freedom in 1795. Within a decade, he was able to obtain the freedom of his slave wife and children. He then turned his attention to business interests that included a barbershop, farms, town property, and slaves. Most of the slaves Stanly owned were field hands, unskilled laborers, and children. In 1830, at the height of his success, Stanly owned around 160 slaves.

Stanly later lost most of his fortune. But while he was alive, he held the respect of the white community. Stanly even owned a pew in the white First Presbyterian Church of New Bern. Even though he himself had been a slave, Stanly's treatment of his slaves differed little from that of white masters. Such were the ironies of what the South called its 'peculiar institution'." (13)

WORDS CONVEY MORE THAN JUST MEANING

Nicole, perhaps you were not aware that there were many "free Negroes" in the South during the period of slavery. If you were, also, not aware that there were so called "Black" slave owners in America or that there were "White" slaves then you were likely misinformed and was ignorant regarding the reality of slavery in America.

Look up the word "Ignorant". It does not mean that you are dumb, stupid, or without high intellect. Being ignorant in this instance is not your fault. It means that you are *"lacking in knowledge or training or being unlearned"*. Likely your ignorance regarding slavery in America is the fault of your ignorant educators in school. They may well have taught you erroneous information and failed in their responsibility to teach accurate and thorough facts because of their lack of knowledge.

The point here is that words do not only have meaning. As mentioned prior, words also capsulize knowledge and comprehension. One person who hears the word "slavery" may mentally process an image of an "African person", while another person, without a racialistic mind-set and with a factual knowledge associated with the word, may process "people" with a mental imagery of both light and dark skinned people. In this case the first person would be ignorant of the facts and racially biased and the second would be simply correctly informed without a racial bias.

Likewise, a person who thinks of "Slave Owners" in America as "White" has an ignorant racist mind-set, most often without even realizing it. So effective has been the "Racialization" of America that the majority of good, even highly educated, people have been made ignorant of the truth and manipulated into thinking in racialistic terms and concepts.

I do not know who orchestrated this ignorance, or why this mental malignance has been allowed to exist, however, I see the destructive effect it is having on my nation and I am deeply saddened and concerned.

As President Abraham Lincoln quoted from the Bible:

" (a) house divided against itself shall not stand". (Matthew 12:25) KJV

Nicole, I suggest that you Google search such words as "Caucasian Slave History". You may well be shocked at the actual truth regarding how "1 million to 1.25 million white Christian Europeans were enslaved in North Africa, from the beginning of the 16th century to the middle of the 18th". (14)

Then perhaps search "White Slaves in America". You might find an article depicting the deplorable enslavement of the Irish noting that "during the 1650s, over 100,000 Irish children between the ages of 10 and 14 were forcibly taken from their parents and sold as slaves in the West Indies, Virginia and New England". (15)

Search "White Child Slave History". You might come across the New York Times article titled "The Young White Faces of Slavery" (16), or read about the "Child Labor in U.S. History" (17).

You can also search for the Wikipedia article on "Anthony Johnson, colonist" (18), for more information about the African man known as "The Black Patriarch", and the "Father of Slavery" in America.

SLAVERY TODAY

Africa has been involved in slavery, with Africans enslaving other Africans and trading their slaves, since "before historical records". That involvement continues until this day.

On the other hand, slavery was so abhorrent to so called "White" people that slavery was abolished in America and Europe in the eighteen hundreds.

The following is quoted from Wikipedia.org with the title:" **Slavery in contemporary Africa**"

"The continent of Africa is one of the most problematic regions in terms of contemporary slavery. Slavery in Africa has a long history, within Africa, since before historical records, but intensifying with the Arab slave trade and again with the trans-Atlantic slave trade; the demand for slaves created an entire series of kingdoms (such as the Ashanti Empire) which existed in a state of perpetual warfare in order to generate the prisoners of war necessary for the lucrative export of slaves. These patterns have persisted into the colonial period during the late 19th and early 20th century. Although the colonial authorities attempted to suppress slavery from about 1900, this had very limited success, and after decolonization, slavery continues in many parts of Africa even though being technically illegal.

Slavery in the Sahel region (and to a lesser extent the Horn of Africa), exist along the racial and cultural boundary of Arabized Berbers in the north and darker Africans in the south. Slavery in the Sahel states of Mauritania, Mali, Niger, Chad and Sudan in particular, continues a centuries-old pattern of hereditary servitude. Other forms of traditional slavery exist in parts of Ghana, Benin, Togo and Nigeria. There are other, non-traditional forms of slavery in Africa today, mostly involving human trafficking and the enslavement of child soldiers and child labourers, e.g. human trafficking in Angola, and human trafficking of children from Togo, Benin and Nigeria to Gabon and Cameroon.

Modern day slavery in Africa according to the Anti-Slavery Society includes exploitation of subjugate populations even when their condition is not technically called 'slavery':

'Although this exploitation is often not called slavery, the conditions are the same. People are sold like objects, forced to work for little or no pay and are at the mercy of their "employers".'
—Antislavery Society, Interview with an indigenous man in the Congo

...Forced labor in Sub-Saharan Africa is estimated at 660,000. This includes people involved in the illegal diamond mines of Sierra Leone and Liberia, which is also a direct result of the civil war in these regions

...Child slave trade: Human trafficking in Nigeria, Human trafficking in Benin, and Human trafficking in Togo

The trading of children has been reported in modern Nigeria and Benin. The children are kidnapped or purchased for $20 – $70 each by slavers in poorer states, such as Benin and Togo, and sold into slavery in sex dens or as unpaid domestic servants for $350.00 each in wealthier oil-rich states, such as Nigeria and Gabon." (19)

African Slavery Participation

In doing some reading regarding the issue of African involvement in the slave trade, I came across a number of articles denying that Africans sold Africans. One article stated that:

> "Africans sold their own people is a stock argument White Americans use when the subject of slavery comes up." (20)

Here, again, the need to place blame on "White" people and the solicitation of "White" guilt supersedes the truth.

In an article titled **"It's Time to Face the Whole Truth about the Atlantic Slave Trade"** by Sheldon M. Stern, the facts are quite clear.

Mr. Stern's credentials include: *"… taught African American history at the college level for a decade before becoming historian at the John F. Kennedy Library and Museum (1977–1999)—where he designed the museum's first civil rights exhibit."*

Mr. Stern begins the article with a quote from Aldous Huxley:

> *"Facts do not cease to exist because they are ignored."*

It is very important to read the entire article because the following fails to explain the full scope and purpose of Mr. Stern's composition. The intention here is only to illustrate how misinformed many are regarding the truth about the slave trade.

Mr. Stern begins by stating the objective of the information is to:

"...improve relationships between races and cultures by acknowledging our common experiences and encouraging dialogue that is based upon respect."

Following are selected quotes:

"Incomplete depictions of the Atlantic slave trade are, in fact, quite common. My 2003 study of 49 state U.S. history standards revealed that not one of these guides to classroom content even mentioned the key role of Africans in supplying the Atlantic slave trade. In Africa itself, however, the slave trade is remembered quite differently. Nigerians, for example, explicitly teach about their own role in the trade:

Where did the supply of slaves come from? First, the Portuguese themselves kidnapped some Africans. But the bulk of the supply came from the Nigerians. These Nigerian middlemen moved to the interior where they captured other Nigerians who belonged to other communities. The middlemen also purchased many of the slaves from the people in the interior . . . . Many Nigerian middlemen began to depend totally on the slave trade and neglected every other business and occupation. The result was that when the trade was abolished [by England in 1807] these Nigerians began to protest. As years went by and the trade collapsed such Nigerians lost their sources of income and became impoverished.

In Ghana, politician and educator Samuel Sulemana Fuseini has acknowledged that his Asante ancestors accumulated their great wealth by abducting, capturing, and kidnapping Africans and selling them as slaves. Likewise, Ghanaian diplomat Kofi Awoonor has written: "I believe there is a great psychic shadow over Africa, and it has much to do with our guilt and denial of our role in the slave trade. We too are blameworthy in what was essentially one of the most heinous crimes in human history.

In 2000, at an observance attended by delegates from several European countries and the United States, officials from Benin publicized President Mathieu Kerekou's apology for his country's role in "selling fellow Africans by the millions to white slave traders." "We cry for forgiveness and reconciliation," said Luc Gnacadja, Benin's minister of environment and housing. Cyrille Oguin, Benin's ambassador to the United States, acknowledged, "We share in the responsibility for this terrible human tragedy."

The article refers to a PBS production with the statement:

"The historical record is incontrovertible—as documented in the PBS Africans in America series companion book:
The white man did not introduce slavery to Africa . . . . And by the fifteenth century, men with dark skin had become quite comfortable with the concept of man as property . . . . Long before the arrival of Europeans on West Africa's coast, the two continents shared a common acceptance of slavery as an unavoidable and necessary—perhaps even desirable—fact of existence. The commerce between the two continents, as tragic as it would become, developed upon familiar territory. Slavery was not a twisted European manipulation,

although Europe capitalized on a mutual understanding and greedily expanded the slave trade into what would become a horrific enterprise . . . . It was a thunder that had no sound. Tribe stalked tribe, and eventually more than 20 million Africans would be kidnapped in their own homeland.

Historians estimate that ten million of these abducted Africans never even made it to the slave ships. Most died on the march to the sea—still chained, yoked, and shackled by their African captors—before they ever laid eyes on a white slave trader. The survivors were either purchased by European slave dealers or instantly beheaded by the African traders in sight of the [slave ship] captain if they could not be sold. Of course, the even more horrific and inhuman middle passage—the voyage of a European (and later American) slave ship from Africa to the Western Hemisphere—still lay before those who had survived the forced trek to the coast."

And finally here, Mr. Stern, supports the contention and purpose of this document:

"Failure to educate young Americans about the whole story of Atlantic slave trade threatens to divide our nation and undermine our civic unity and belief in the historical legitimacy of our democratic institutions. Education in a democracy cannot promote half-truths about history without undermining the ideal of e pluribus unum— one from many—and substituting a divisive emphasis on many from one. The history of the slave trade proves

that virtually everyone participated and profited—whites and blacks; Christians, Muslims, and Jews; Europeans, Africans, Americans, and Latin Americans. Once we recognize the shared historical responsibility for the Atlantic slave trade, we can turn our attention to "transforming the future" by eradicating its corrosive legacy." (21)

(To read the full article go to: http://historynewsnetwork.org/article/41431)

Vilification

The issues of Slavery and Race have been used for some time to vilify so called "White" people. This might have contributed to your feelings of dislike for "White" people based on what you have been told or learned in school. The information and facts presented prior in this writing are either ignored or unknown by, perhaps, the majority of people in our nation.

Conversely, this is not to vilify, in any way, people with African heritage. Knowing the truth is essential in resolving issues. We have to join together as American citizens in dispelling racial ignorance and rise together as one nation without residual blame and accusation. To quote the biblical verse John 8:32,

> *"And ye shall know the truth, and the truth shall make you free"*.

Again, many educators are programed mentally to think in terms of "White" and "Black" erroneous racial generalities, as are many well-meaning people in America. This subliminal prejudice and bigotry infuses their minds with myths and half-truths that are unsupported by fact, but forms a consensus of opinion generally. This effects both educators and textbook authors in disseminating counterfactual information regarding ethnological issues.

For this reason history regarding these issues has been falsified to support the presuppositions of people who think in terms of racialistic stereotypes and suffer from an obsessive emphasis on racial group classifications and categories rather than individual citizens.

Singularity

Nicole, people are individuals. Each person is a unique entity with varied and distinct characteristics. Life is a single experience. No one but ourselves know our thoughts, no one but ourselves know our pain, no one but ourselves feel our emotions. As Lao Tsu wrote,

"I am alone with the beating of my heart."

Let me stress again, we should think of every American Citizen, and human, as an individual without preconceived notions. When we meet a person that we have no prior knowledge or experience with, we should think of them only as an individual person, nothing more.

We should greet that individual without projecting mentally that the person is "Black", "White", or whatever racial hue, along with any prejudgments we associate with that racial classification. We should then begin to relate and consider that person by only our experience with that individual alone.

It can begin with a smile, a grimace or vacant expression. A person might be friendly and personable, unfriendly and rude, or perhaps, detached and noninvolved. In every case, our opinion of that person should be based exclusively on our experience.

There are exceptions to that, of course, by necessity. Some examples would be persons in declared conflict, persons in mob confrontations, and persons who group themselves in contrary positions to the civil order. It is difficult to relate to an individual that presents themselves as part of an organization or grouping that precludes individualism and imposes some ideology on you as an individual.

For example, our nation does not declare war on single individuals and assigns individual identity to a classification of "enemy". Also at times people present themselves as indivisible from a larger body. In such cases, it is impossible to relate to these persons as unclassified individuals since they lose their individuality in being part of the conglomerate.

Ultimately, however, we must come together as fully enfranchised individual citizens united under the Constitution and Bill of Rights which assures our individual freedom.

This is what makes America unique. America subscribes to the doctrines of Individualism and Democracy which relate to the emphasis on, and eminence of, the individual citizen.

INDIVIDUALISM

The concept and principal of individual rights is fundamental for freedom and personal liberty. Racialistic thinking, and polarization into groups by skin color only, is the antithesis of individualism.

Because much social progress has been made by individuals forming groups untied for mutual benefit, organized initiatives and efforts are essential. Ultimately, however, the individual cannot be fully enfranchised as an individual citizen until they move beyond group identity in their personal lives. Certainly, they can use the union to obtain defined objectives, however, they must realize their individual identity beyond the group to fully experience and enjoy the freedom of being their individual self without racial encumbrance.

Hopefully, one day, we will achieve a nation of individual American Citizens, plain and simple, with no divisions, or qualifications.

"Individualism is the moral stance, political philosophy, ideology, or social outlook that emphasizes the moral worth of the individual. Individualists promote the exercise of one's goals and desires and so value independence and self-reliance and advocate that interests of the individual should achieve precedence over the state or a social group, while opposing external interference upon one's own interests by society or institutions such as the government. Individualism is often defined in contrast to totalitarianism, collectivism and more corporate social forms.

Individualism makes the individual its focus and so starts with the fundamental premise that the human individual is of primary importance in the struggle for liberation... Individualism thus involves the right of the individual to freedom and self-realization." (22)

DEMOCRACY

Individual freedom begins with the concept and principal of Democracy. Here, again, we form political unions to forward our desires and objectives from the government we elect. In the area of race, Democracy has given us "Civil Rights Legislation" that was passed by the majority to protect a minority among us.

Democracy has proven to be the best way known for the individual to participate in government. But, once again, the individual citizen should strive to think independently beyond a political party and vote their conscience for the good of the Nation, not the political organization.

From Wikipedia.org searching Democracy:

"Democracy in modern usage, is a system of government in which the citizens exercise power directly or elect representatives from among themselves to form a governing body, such as a parliament.

According to political scientist Larry Diamond, democracy consists of four key elements: A political system for choosing and replacing the government through free and fair elections; The active participation of the people, as citizens, in politics and civic life; Protection of the human rights of all citizens, and A rule of law, in which the laws and procedures apply equally to all citizens." (23)

LIBERTY

Not only did the French give America the Statue of Liberty, now in the New York Harbor, but they also contributed to the world the principles, symbolized by the Stature, that resulted in the doctrine of individual liberty for all human beings. The love and demand for personal Liberty is the catalyst that led to the achievement of freedom over arbitrary or despotic government in Europe and Colonial America. As Patrick Henry said in 1775, *"Give me liberty, or give me death!"*

Dedicated in 1886, shortly after the end of the Civil War, the statue represents Libertas, the Roman goddess. She holds a torch high over her head representing Liberty Enlightening the world with freedom of the individual human being.

She holds a tablet with a book of laws representing the principles of individual liberty. The date of America's Declaration of Independence, July 4, 1776, is inscribed on the tablet. The concept of, *"We hold these truths to be self-evident, that all men are created equal, that among these are Life, Liberty and the Pursuit of Happiness"*, express the principles implied by the tablet.

Her crown has seven spikes representing the 7 seas and continents of the world indicating the universal nature of individual freedom.

At her feet are broken chains representing freedom of the individual from government oppression and slavery. She is there to remind us that we all, equally, bask in the light of Liberty.

The Age of Enlightenment

The concepts of individual liberty and government, by and for the people, were spawned in the period known as the "Age of Enlightenment". It is important to be aware of this history in order to understand the roots of American culture and the foundation of our heritage as American Citizens.

Nicole, when you think of "White" people, understand that the people you dislike gave these guiding principles to you and the world. To achieve this, there was great struggle and loss of life. However, today, we are so secure in these principles of freedom that we take them for granted without any consideration or appreciation.

Unfortunately, this apathy can foreshadow our losing these principles in the future.

"Enlightenment was an intellectual movement which dominated the world of ideas in Europe in the 18th century. The Enlightenment included a range of ideas centered on reason as the primary source of authority and legitimacy, and came to advance ideals such as liberty, progress, tolerance, fraternity, constitutional government, and separation of church and state. In France, the central doctrines of les Lumières were individual liberty and religious tolerance in opposition to an absolute monarchy and the fixed dogmas of the Roman Catholic Church.

...Benjamin Franklin visited Europe repeatedly and contributed actively to the scientific and political debates there and brought the newest ideas back to Philadelphia. Thomas Jefferson closely followed European ideas and later incorporated some of the ideals of the Enlightenment

into the Declaration of Independence (1776). Others like James Madison incorporated them into the Constitution in 1787." (24)

More specifically to America:

"The **American Enlightenment** is a period of intellectual ferment in the thirteen American colonies in the period 1714–1818, which led to the American Revolution, and the creation of the American Republic. Influenced by the 18th-century European Enlightenment and its own Native American philosophy, the American Enlightenment applied scientific reasoning to politics, science, and religion, promoted religious tolerance, and restored literature, the arts, and music as important disciplines and professions worthy of study in colleges.

..Enlightened Founding Fathers, especially Benjamin Franklin, Thomas Jefferson, James Madison and George Washington, fought for and eventually attained religious freedom for minority denominations. According to the founding fathers, the United States should be a country where peoples of all faiths could live in peace and mutual benefit. James Madison summed up this ideal in 1792 saying, "Conscience is the most sacred of all property.

...Between 1714 and 1818 a great intellectual change took place that changed the British Colonies of America from a distant backwater into a leader in the fields of moral philosophy, educational reform, religious revival, industrial technology, science, and, most notably, political *philosophy. It saw a consensus on a "pursuit of happiness" based political philosophy".* (25)

People such as John Adams, James Madison, James Wilson, Ethan Allen, Alexander Hamilton, Benjamin Franklin, Thomas Jefferson, and George Washington, to name just a few of the free thinkers of the period, dreamed the dream of American Liberty and fought to establish the principles of individual Liberty you experience today, Nicole, as an American Citizen.

Yet I have heard and read references to these noble individuals with expressions like "old white men who enslaved people". A person that could reduce the benefactors of our great nation to such a demeaning choice of words must be blinded by acute racialism and be mentally impaired by extreme historical ignorance.

First of all, the majority of "these old white men" were actually relativity young at the time of the Revolutionary War on July 4, 1776: James Monroe, 18; Alexander Hamilton, 21; Aaron Burr, 20; Betsy Ross, 24; James Madison, 25; Thomas Jefferson, 33; John Adams, 40; Paul Revere, 41; George Washington, 44.

And, yes, a racialist classification would stereotype them as "White" or Caucasian. They were primarily of European ancestry with ideas, practices and attitudes toward individual human rights very different than many other peoples with different shades of skin color. However, it was enlightened people such as these that established the intellectual seeds that resulted in the movement to abolish slavery in America and throughout the civilized world.

All who enjoy personal liberty today, throughout the world, must attribute the freedom they enjoy and experience today to

these "light skinned people" who orchestrated and demand-
ed the concepts of individual human dignity and liberty be
established.

The concepts of Personal Liberty and Individual Freedom are
nonracial and inclusive of all human beings.

I would say to the person who would reduce and define
America's founding fathers and mothers as *"Old and White"*:

*Measure the value of your own life and your contribution to
humankind against the value of their lives and the contribution
these "Old White Men" made to humanity. See how you measure up in comparison. Perhaps a measure of appreciation for
what they contributed to your life would increase your own value
and standing as a human being. There is perhaps nothing lower
in measure than an ingrate who disparages the heroes that risk
their lives to set them free.*

AMERICA'S FOUNDING MOTHERS

Actually the person using the term "Old White Men" to define and refer to the people who participated in the struggle to fight and establish the United States of America, express another ignorance as well as their racialistic bias. The self-satisfaction they might feel in seeking to belittle men of such high esteem is betrayed by their obvious lack of knowledge regarding the founding of our country.

Guess what, there were women around during the time of the Revolution...intelligent, proactive, resourceful and essential individuals that made vital contributions to this momentous achievement.

> "Everyone's heard of Paul Revere, George Washington, Benedict Arnold, and Peyton Randolph, but who knows about Molly Pitcher, Penelope Barker, Esther Reed, or Patience Wright? Well, if you haven't, you've come to the right place. Not all of them picked up muskets. Some chose to fight with an arrow or a cannon. Others chose a pen, a needle, a pitchfork, sculpting tools, and an apron. Some of these women fought up close. One contributed from thousands of miles away. But, if it weren't for these women, we might be singing My country Tis of Thee with its original lyrics." (26)

You can read about some of the women who contributed to the revolution from a list at this link which is the source of the quote above:

Go to: http://score.rims.k12.ca.us./ Look under "Directories" for "Lesson Directory" / From the drop down menu select "women_american_revolution"

FURTHER ACCUSATION

Of course the racialistic description of America's Founding Fathers and Mothers also includes the imputation that they "enslaved people". According to his depiction, they were not only "Old", "White" and "Men"; they were also "Slave Masters".

Nicole, I have no defense or tolerance for enslaving another human being. I deeply believe that all people are created, by the very source of the Universe, as equal individuals regardless of where they are born and regardless of gender. I hold personal Liberty and Individual Freedom to be the paramount achievement of civilization.

Without any equivocation, the act of slavery was, is and will always be immoral and inhumane.

The only way I can address this issue regarding people like George Washington owning slaves is to consider the way slavery was introduced in the early American colonies and to consider what might be mitigating circumstances associated with the atrocity. I cannot justify the practice, and have to take solace only in that the practice was so abhorrent to enough people, at that time, to eventually abolish slavery in America. Even George Washington was uncomfortable with the practice of slavery:

"After the war, Washington often privately expressed a dislike of the institution of slavery. In 1786, he wrote to a friend that "I never mean ... to possess another slave by purchase; it being among my first wishes to see some plan adopted, by which slavery in this Country may be abolished by slow, sure and imperceptible degrees." To another friend he wrote that "there is not a man living who wishes more sincerely than I do to see some plan adopted for the abolition of slavery." (27)

Washington grew up when owning slaves was acceptable. When he was *"eleven years old, he inherited ten slaves"*. While this does not justify his participating in the practice, it does indicate that this was not a thoughtful or considered decision as an adult to subscribe to this vile practice.

The way I evaluate the situation is to consider what Washington and the other Founding Fathers and Mothers contributed to the world, and to we as a nation, today. I also have to consider that Slavery was not acceptable and eventually was abolished. While we continue today to enjoy the benefits of what the Founding Fathers and Mothers accomplished at that time, the deplorable aspect of Slavery was not allowed to exist in our time.

To further put slavery in the context of that period, we need to understand how much of the American Colonies were settled.

Indentured Servitude (Debt Slavery)

Over half of the initial settlers coming to the American Colonies were debt slaves.

> "Between the 1630's and the American Revolution, one-half to two thirds of white immigrants to the Thirteen Colonies arrived under indentures.
>
> ...Before the Civil War, slaves and indentured servants were considered personal property, and they or their descendants could be sold or inherited like any other property. Like other property, human chattel was governed largely by laws of individual states. Generally, these laws concerning indentured servants and slaves did not differentiate between the sexes. Some, however, addressed only women. Regardless of their country of origin, many early immigrants were indentured servants, people who sold their labor in exchange for passage to the New World and housing on their arrival." (28)

In fact, this is the way that initial Africans arrived in America, with the exception that they were most likely traded rather than killed by African tribes that were holding them captive. Had the initial colonists not been willing to pay for their passage from Africa and put them in indentured servitude, they would have surely died on the ships.

We have looked into some of the history of slavery prior in this writing, however, it is important to understand how Indentured Servitude changed in time to Chattel Slavery.

An outline from "The History of Slavery in America" from Berkley University gives this brief timeline for the change:

* ⁜ **"Gradual Change of Status.** *There was a gradual change in the status of African Americans from indentured servants to chattel slaves.*
* ⁜ **1640 Virginia Courts.** *In 1640, the Virginia courts had sentenced one of the first black indentured servants to slavery.*
* ⁜ **John Casor.** *In 1654, John Casor became the first legal slave in America. Anthony Johnson, previously an African indentured slave, claimed John Casor as his slave. The Northampton County Court ruled against Casor, and declared him propter for life by Anthony Johnson. Since Africans were not English, they were not covered by the English Common Law."*

Eventually, however, the worst part of humanity prevailed for some in Southern America:

"Initially, most laws passed concerned indentured servants, but around the middle of the seventeenth century, colonial laws began to reflect differences between indentured servants and slaves. More important, the laws began to differentiate between races: the association of 'servitude for natural life' with people of African descent became common. Re Negro John Punch (1640) was one of the early cases that made a racial distinction among indentured servants." (28)

It may have been Anthony Johnson, an African, who owned the *"first legal slave in America"*, however, many of the other colonists, particularly in the South, were just as complicit in institutionalizing the chattel slavery system. For some people, the benefits of captive "free labor" was a victory of greed and evil over good conscious morality.

The broad acceptance of indentured servitude, and the fact that it had been beneficial to many poor "Black" and "White" people arriving at the American shores in desperate condition, had made the change to actual slavery incremental rather than abrupt. Many likely rationalized that the Africans were "better off" being slaves in America than what their circumstances would have been in their African homeland.

Of course this was wrong and was intolerable to many in the Colonies.

ABOLITION

Actually there was never a time when Chattel Slavery was acceptable to many of the Colonists.

The Abolition movement began immediately with the implementation of legal chattel slavery. At a time when there was no way for Africans to effectively object to being enslaved, many people you would consider "White" adamantly objected to the practice and ultimately, in the Civil War, took up arms to abolish Slavery in the new American nation.

> "The historian James M. McPherson defines an abolitionist "as one who before the Civil War had agitated for the immediate, unconditional, and total abolition of slavery in the United States." He does not include antislavery activists such as Abraham Lincoln or the Republican Party, which called for the gradual ending of slavery.
>
> The first attempts to end slavery in the British/American colonies came from Thomas Jefferson and some of his contemporaries. Despite the fact that Jefferson was a lifelong slaveholder, he included strong anti-slavery language in the original draft of the Declaration of Independence, but other delegates took it out. Benjamin Franklin, also a slaveholder for most of his life, was a leading member of the Pennsylvania Society for the Abolition of Slavery, the first recognized organization for abolitionists in the United States. Following the Revolutionary War, Northern states abolished slavery, beginning with the 1777 constitution of Vermont, followed by Pennsylvania's gradual emancipation act in 1780. Other states with more of an economic interest in slaves, such as New York and New Jersey, also

passed gradual emancipation laws, and by 1804, all the northern states had abolished it. Some slaves continued in servitude for two more decades but most were freed.

Also in the postwar years, individual slaveholders, particularly in the Upper South, manumitted slaves, sometimes in their wills. Many noted they had been moved by the revolutionary ideals of the equality of men. The number of free blacks as a proportion of the black population increased from less than one per cent to nearly ten per cent from 1790 to 1810 in the Upper South as a result of these actions.

As President, on 2 March 1807, Jefferson signed the Act Prohibiting Importation of Slaves and it took effect in 1808, which was the earliest allowed under the Constitution. In 1820 he privately supported the Missouri Compromise, believing it would help to end slavery. He left the anti-slavery struggle to younger men after that." (29)

Ultimately over 600,000 lives, mostly what would now be called "White", were lost in deciding the issue for our new Nation. An article titled Death and Dying, written by Drew Gilpin Faust for the National Park Service gives a dismal description of the carnage that resulted:

"In the middle of the 19th century, the United States entered into a civil war that proved bloodier than any other conflict in American history, a war that would presage the slaughter of World War I's Western Front and the global carnage of the 20th century. The number of soldiers

who died between 1861 and 1865, generally estimated at 620,000, is approximately equal to the total of American fatalities in the Revolutionary War, the War of 1812, the Mexican War, the Spanish American War, World War I, World War II, and the Korean War, combined. The Civil War's rate of death, its incidence in comparison with the size of the American population, was six times that of World War II. A similar rate, about two percent, in the United States today would mean six million fatalities. As the new southern nation struggled for survival against a wealthier and more populous enemy, its death toll reflected the disproportionate strains on its human capital. Confederate men died at a rate three times that of their Yankee counterparts; one in five white southern men of military age did not survive the Civil War. Twice as many Civil War soldiers died from disease as from battle wounds, the result in considerable measure of poor sanitation in an era that created mass armies that did not yet understand the transmission of infectious diseases like typhoid, typhus, and dysentery.

These military statistics, however, tell only a part of the story. The war also killed a significant number of civilians; battles raged across farm and field, encampments of troops spread epidemic disease, guerrillas ensnared women and children in violence and reprisals, draft rioters targeted innocent citizens, and shortages of food in parts of the South brought starvation. No one sought to document these deaths systematically, and no one has devised a method of undertaking a retrospective count. The distinguished Civil War historian James McPherson *has estimated that there were 50,000 civilian deaths dur-ing the war, and has concluded that the overall mortality rate for the South exceeded that of any country in World War I and all but the region between the Rhine and the Volga in World War II. The American Civil War produced carnage that was often thought to be reserved for the combination of technological proficiency and inhumanity characteristic of a later time."* (30)

Slavery was finally abolished at a devastating cost for our new Nation.

Nicole, would you have hated the "White" soldiers in the North that lost their lives in the conflict? Do you feel that the "White" people in the South suffered enough in loss of life?

Can we consider the treatment of, so called, "Black" people from that era resolved? Does the fact that relatively few, so called, "Black" lives were taken in the struggle to set them free, help re-habilitate your resentment of "White" people? Isn't it about time that we reconcile as free Citizens in America with an appreciation of what was paid in human life and suffering to abolish Slavery in this Nation?

AFTER THE CIVIL WAR

Firstly, there was no stereotypical results or behavior. What can be said is that so called "people of color" in the northern states continued to be as free as before. The "Black" and "White" slave owners lost their right to have slaves.

In the Southern States the Democratic Party resisted the efforts of the Republican Party from the Northern States in their efforts to implement the provisions of the Emancipation Proclamation that set the Slaves Free. The Republicans came to the South to help the "Free Negros" take positions as Citizens and participate in the government.

Keep in mind that the people from the Northern States were what you would call "White". They were determined to force the "White" people in the Southern States to give the former slaves an equal status as citizens.

It is difficult to lump "White" people of this era in a single racial grouping since some wanted to continue Slavery, while other "Whites" were insisting that the "Blacks" be set free.

There was much resistance and, in some cases, criminal response by some of the "White" Southerners. There was certainly horrendous atrocities. In some cases there was criminal activity by some of the newly freed "Black" Southerners.

The Southern resistance is complicated by the fact that some people in the South were trying to recover from the devastation of war and retain some vestige of their culture while at the same time having to accept civic integration of the more primitive African culture.

Of course, the people in the South that had held Slaves, kept the Africans uneducated and in more primitive conditions which was deplorable and denied them the opportunity to advance culturally. However, the majority of the people in the South had not owned slaves and were extremely reluctant to accept them as equal citizens. They were wrong and they had no choice.

Nicole, you can learn more about what is called the "Reconstruction" that took place in the Southern States after the Civil War to learn more about the struggle to overcome the abomination of slavery.

However, the inexorable progress toward full freedom for all people continues, at times slowly, at times by forced compliance...but the trend was, and is, in the right direction. This is a testament to the determination of the American people to fulfill the guiding principles of Liberty for all individuals. Our founding Fathers and Mothers would certainly be saddened by the strife and suffering of the Civil War, however, they would be proud that we are still heading in the direction they established by our Constitution and Bill or Rights. I truly feel that if we can now abandon the animosity, resentment, and envy we hold toward others, as well as the distrust and prejudice; we can begin to coalesce into a nation of united individuals.

This would be a lot to overcome. A people divided by animosity, resentment, envy, distrust and prejudice, just to name the primary reasons for division, are far more likely to stay conflicted. A state or turmoil and disorder, if not actually civil war or external destruction, is far more likely to occur.

The forces of division now rule in our Country. We would have to confront government and social instigators that have us convinced that we cannot make it as individuals together and that our only strength is in the racial and social divides. Many feel that without our racial grouping or our political polarization we would surely return to chaos and injustice.

As individuals, we seem not to want a nation of advancement and achievement of the fittest, best and most capable regardless of race. We seem not to want to apply the principles we impose on sports to be imposed on our "real" lives. We seem not to want the individual to be challenged to obtain their personal best. We seem not to expect the individual to accept responsibility for their character and personal actions. We do not trust each other to respect the rights of their fellow citizens as we join hands and hearts to make our Nation the best, most free and most prosperous country in the World.

Many seem to feel that the commitment to individual liberty, freedom, equality and the pursuit of happiness does not exist in the people today without racial polarization. Many seem to fear that the driving forces that caused good people to rise up against the injustice of slavery being experienced by the weakest among them about 200 years ago in America, is now dead. We seem to ignore the fact there are Americans today, across all racial divides, who readily stand up to demand equal human rights. Many fear to trust in The Constitution and Bill or Rights as guiding principles for our nation and the government "of the people" we elect. Maybe we trust in God but not in our brother and sister Citizens.

So we expect the worst from one another…and we get what we expect. Unless we change, we will surely get what we anticipate. Nicole, a very wise man once said:

"If you change yourself, you will change your world. If you change how you think then you will change how you feel and what actions you take. And so the world around you will change."
—Mahatma Gandhi

SEGREGATION

Perhaps one of the most misunderstood, at times divisive, yet often benign social dispositions is segregation. It is a natural social tendency that is as inclusive as exclusive. It can, however, lead to unacceptable social injustice if allowed to be pervasive in the public communal.

Someone once pointed out to me that there is one hour each week that is the most segregated period of time throughout America. This is national segregation that is voluntary and by mutual choice. No one objects and people feel it is an integral part of our Freedom.

The most segregated hour takes place in churches. People can freely go to any church of their choice. No one guards the door, no one would, or should, feel anyone is not welcome to attend. Yet people segregate themselves at their own preference.

Most often the voluntary segregation is along racial, ethnic and cultural associations. Should the government require that this form of segregation be outlawed and require that the groups integrate in representative equal and diverse numbers distributed over the available church options, there would be an uproar and a social revolt. It would likely not be acceptable to anyone and most people would likely refuse to adhere to the new law.

This explains, but does not justify, how people have reacted to forced integration.

I recall, as a young person, when right and good sense led the government in the South to force integration of schools. At that time the justification was that the schools were "separate but equal". I do not know if they were equal in educational quality, but suspect that there were not in many aspects.

It made good sense to me that we should all be one people without racial division. Yet there was a great deal of resistance to the change, but not to the degree we would have in forceful integration of our churches.

Over time, however, I have been disappointed that the integration has been circumvented. In some measure I actually resent the hypocrisy of noncompliance by some of the people.

Today we have "Black" Colleges that are racially justified as being "historically black". They are not actually integrated. We have a "Black" television channel, "Black" beauty contests, "Black" Lives Matter, "Black" this and "Black" that. One way to determine if these are racialistic institutions is to consider what would be said if there were "Historically White" colleges with very few "Black" students, or perhaps a "White" TV Channel or Beauty Pageant. I'm sure there are racialistic rationalizations, however, the reality is pure racialism and the perpetuation of institutionalized segregation. This lack of diversity and integration should be abandoned for the good of our nation.

The feelings I had for those so called "White" people who wanted to retain the exclusive cultural and racial identity of segregated schools in the past are the same feelings I have now. Integration may be distasteful for the "Black" institutions, however, it is the right thing to do and absolutely necessary for the homogeny of our nation for the same reasons it was necessary before. There is no acceptable difference.

Culture

Ethnic Culture is a different issue and extremely complicated. The acceptable tradition in America has been to subordinate ethnic culture to shared American Culture. Since America is an ethnic and cultural conglomerate, there is actually no single fundamental ethnicity or culture other than the assimilation of our Nation's founding principles.

We have a tendency to celebrate and participate together in a variety of cultural events. St Patricks' Day is enjoyed not only by the Irish, but often cheerfully acknowledged by many not of Irish ancestry. I often go to the local Greek Festival and enjoy the delicious baklava.

America, then, is a multi-cultural society that unite under the mantel of being American Citizens. It is only when the individual emphasizes ethnicity and culture above national identity that ethnic culture becomes divisive and unacceptable.

This is one reason why some people feel that we need a single language in the Nation as a unifying factor.

As long as we are Americans first and foremost, and are willing to forsake these subordinate identities for national unity, then the celebration of ethnic culture is something we can all share and celebrate together. Otherwise, a citizen cannot be fully enfranchised when their allegiance is divided or secondary because of ethnic culture.

DISCRIMINATION

In the context of race relations, discrimination has become a derogatory word. It implies the "making of a distinction in favor or against a person based on group, class or category". It literally defines the concept of racial stereotyping with a demeaning bias.

However, as with "segregation", we all discriminate in the broader sense of the word. We all "note or observe a difference and distinction" in many situations and circumstances. We discriminate to determine between what is good or bad, lawful or unlawful, pleasant or unpleasant. Our mental process may be corrupted by bias or prejudice, but the act of discrimination is essential to our making judgements and decisions and, at times, to our very survival.

We discriminate regarding who we invite into our homes. If the government required that we put a sign outside our home that read something like this: "We do not discriminate between our fellow citizens as friends, all who would wish to visit may, and they will be invited into our home, as friends, without our making any distinctions".

This is only to make a point and actually sounds ridiculous, of course. The criminals would annihilate us in a short time. I can imagine what society would be like under such conditions. It would be intolerable and we would, of course, refuse to adhere to such a ridiculous law.

So it becomes a matter of when discrimination is acceptable, unacceptable or absolutely necessary.

If someone is rude or intimidating, then I would naturally ostracize them. People who try to force an ideology I don't agree with are not welcome to my time or presence. A person, or people, who feels I am guilty of some past grievance, not perpetrated by myself, are subject to acute discrimination on my part because of their attitude.

RACIAL SUPREMACIST

I searched both "White" Supremacist and "Black" Supremacist in consideration of this segment. As I expected the definition of each is extremely similar. What I know about both is the absurdity of the concept. I feel that if you put all the Supremacist together in a dark pit and only listened to their rhetoric, it would be very difficult to tell them apart except for the use of "White" and "Black". In fact, it is reasonable, I feel, to describe them as being in the same dark racist pit of ignorance and idiocy

I know personally that people who consider themselves as "White Supremacist" are an embarrassment to most people you would call "White". I feel sure that the feeling is mutual for many people of African heritage for people who consider themselves "Black Supremacist".

My writing here was sparked by an article I came across from one of the primary, so called, "Black" Supremacist and Nationalist. Louis Farrakhan is the leader of the Nation of Islam in America with upwards of 50,000 followers. Quoting from an AP article dated December 18, 2016 with the headline "Farrakhan Sees a New Opening for Black Separatist Message":

"In a speech before the State of the Black World Conference in New Jersey, he warned, 'The white man is going to push. He's putting in place the very thing that will limit the freedom of others' Then he pointed to the crowd, smiled and said, 'That's what you needed as motivation to finally separate from whites'.

'My message to Mr. Trump: Push it real good,' Farrakhan said, building to a roar that drew applause and

cheers. 'Push it so good that black people say, 'I'm outta here. I can't take it no more.'" (31)

He is also quoted as saying:

"White people are potential humans - they haven't evolved yet." (32)

This is just an example of how racism has no color. It can be ugly and it can cause violence, however, it is a social disease that has no racial, ethnic or gender barriers. It is important to understand and realize that people are more similar than different... even when it comes to racialism and bigotry.

Had I been raised on what is called an "Indian Reservation" I realize that I would be a very different person today. I might be extremely resentful toward the "European invaders" and full of racialistic animosity. The fact is, our racialistic differences, as people, are far more socially influenced than biological.

ABUSE

Nicole, you mentioned that "White people treat Black People badly". I assume you mean "abusively". Unfortunately I have to challenge the racialism of your statement, yet expand the charge to include humanity itself. Some people treat some other people badly and abusively, and this has been going on for all of human history.

However, since you were specific in your allegation, then I will be somewhat specific in responding to your charge.

As I write this, a young "White" man was just found guilty of going into a church in Charleston, South Carolina and shooting 9 of the members who were "Black". The nine people died. This atrocity seems to be what is called a racist "hate" crime. This certainly more than supports your assertion. I am reminded of the atrocities attributed to the Ku Klux Klan, a racist "White Supremacists" group, that formed back in the South immediately following the Civil War's end. I have read that "Negros" were even hung from trees in an attempt to intimidate other former slaves who were exerting their newly obtained freedom.

This reminds me of stories I have heard regarding the atrocities perpetrated on the pre-American Native people now called "Indians". There is one where the US Army took blankets from the hospital ward filled with Small Pox patients and gave them to the "Indians".

Another was about the horrible brutality of a US Army group known as the "Buffalo Soldiers". The "Buffalo Soldiers" were a U.S. Cavalry Regiment made up only of men now called "Blacks".

The story was about a Shawnee Clan that had helped many lost Negro slaves trying to reach the North for freedom. It seems some of the escaping Negros were following the North Star which did not actually lead in the northeast direction they needed to follow. When the Shawnee hunters would come across them they would take them for a ways in the right direction and explain how to navigate to their objective, often giving them supplies for the journey.

In one case described, the Buffalo Soldiers attacked one Shawnee encampment that had been so helpful to the escaped slaves. The attack came just after sunrise on the encampment that was filled with only old people, women and children. The men were away in battle. The "Black Soldiers" are said to have murdered the old people and some children and raped some of the women without any show of mercy. They burned the encampment and left the devastated wounded to suffer and deal with the dead bodies.

Unfortunately, history is replete with unimaginably heinous atrocities. You will likely learn about the genocide of the Jewish people by the Nazis during World War II. This is the dark side of humanity and it is not racial or related to skin color. It exist in the most primal part of human nature.

So what I point out following is just another isolated example of humans treating other humans badly, however, in this case I am dealing with your charge that "Whites" treat "Blacks" badly.

First you seem to be referring to the present. To respond I searched "White on "Black Violence" and "Black on White Violence" in an attempt to establish who treats whom more badly. I suggest you do this for yourself to make your own determinations.

I first came across two Videos which were taken off YouTube but were retained by this website. I have listed the source and link following this quote so you can see them if you wish. The text with the videos read:

"Shocking video out of Chicago shows a mob of young black men viciously beating an older white man because he voted for Donald Trump, dragging him through the streets as he hangs out of the back of his car.

The clip shows the thugs repeatedly screaming, 'you voted Donald Trump' as they assault the victim from every angle while others steal his belongings.

'You voted Trump,' the mob screams, 'You gonna pay for that sh*t.'

Another woman shouts 'beat his ass,' while another man is heard laughing before remarking, 'Don't vote Trump.'

(It continues with description of the second video.)

A second video of the incident which is dubbed with the 'F**k Donald Trump' song, a phrase now being chanted by "protesters" across the country, shows one of the attackers driving away in the man's vehicle while his hand is still stuck in the window as the car drags him down the street.

'The scene is frankly reminiscent of a lynching,' remarks Chris Menahan.

It is not even clear if the victim was a Trump supporter. Presumably, the mob used that as an excuse to beat and rob him.

YouTube quickly deleted the video, but it has been mirrored on numerous different websites." (33)

(You can view the videos by going to www.infowars.com and search: Black mob viciously beats white trump voter)

As I was finishing this writing, a horrendous example of human depravity and people you call "Black" abusing a so called "White" person has filled the news. The headline reads: *Chicago torture video: 4 charged with hate crimes, kidnapping*". The perpetrators streamed the brutality on facebook, so there is a video of the atrocity at the link given in the reference.

> *"(CNN) Four suspects have been charged in connection with the attack on a special-needs teen that was streamed on Facebook Live.*
>
> *Video of the attack shows the 18-year-old victim cowering in a corner of a room, tied up with his mouth bound in plastic. His eyes exude fear as his attackers get ready for their next act.*
>
> *One assailant slashes his sweatshirt with a knife. The young woman streaming the abuse on Facebook Live repeatedly turns the camera back to herself.*
>
> *An attacker then takes a knife to the victim's head, carving a patch off his scalp.*
>
> *For the next 25 minutes, the abuse continues for the world to see. The victim is repeatedly kicked and punched, but his screams are apparently ignored.*
>
> *The young woman broadcasting the attack appears dismayed that she's not getting more attention online.*
>
> *Video of the torture has stunned the country, not just because of the graphic abuse, but because of the comments made by some of the assailants.*
>
> *'*F*ck Donald Trump!' one attacker shouted in the video. 'F*ck white people!'*

'Y'all not even commenting on my s***,' she tells a friend during the live stream.

The teen was tied up for four or five hours, Cmdr. Kevin Duffin of the Chicago Police Department told reporters. The victim will recover from his injuries and is at home with his parents, police said." (34)

I think you will agree that these videos are of "Black" people treating a "White" person very badly.

However, your statement that "White people treat Black people badly" is a generalization in nature and not specific to individual incidents. So I will make further points regarding general, statistical facts, not isolated individual cases. Again I am not trying to demonize people you call "Black". I am responding because you seem to be demonizing specifically "White" people and I can only challenge this by showing that, in fact, the acting badly is mutual and is different only in timeframe, situation and degree.

Following is some Department Of Justice statics for the 2012-2013 period:

"Heather Mac Donald of the Manhattan Institute has just published a table of statistics on race and violent crime that she received from the Department of Justice. For the first time in figures of this kind, DOJ has treated Hispanics as a separate category rather than lumping them in with whites. These data cover all violent crimes except murder, but the number of murders is tiny compared to other violent crimes.

This table can be used for a number of interesting calculations. First, we find that during the 2012/2013 period, blacks committed an average of 560,600 violent crimes against whites, whereas whites committed only 99,403 such crimes against blacks. This means blacks were the attackers in 84.9 percent of the violent crimes involving blacks and whites. This figure is consistent with reports from 2008, the last year DOJ released similar statistics. Perhaps not coincidentally, that was the year Mr. Obama was elected president.

Interestingly, we find that violent interracial crime involving blacks and Hispanics occurs in almost exactly the same proportions as black/white crime: Blacks are the attackers 82.5 percent of the time, while Hispanics are attackers only 17.5 percent of the time.

Using figures for the 2013 racial mix of the population–62.2 percent white, 17.1 percent Hispanic, 13.2 percent black–we can calculate the average likelihood of a person of each race attacking the other. A black is 27 times more likely to attack a white and 8 times more likely to attack a Hispanic than the other way around. A Hispanic is eight times more likely to attack a white than vice versa.

We can also calculate how often criminals of each group choose victims of other races. As indicated below, when whites commit violence they choose fellow whites as victims 82.4 percent of the time, and almost never attack blacks. Blacks attack whites almost as often as they attack blacks, and Hispanics attack whites more often than they attack any other group, including their own." (35)

So, Nicole, statistically, a "Black" person is 27 times more likely to treat a "White" person badly, than vice versa. Henceforth, your assertion is incorrect as well as racialistic.

Let's drop the racial aspect of this and say that people, at times, treat other people badly and try to refrain from this practice in our personal life. Respect your fellow citizen as you would have them respect you is a good admonishment for all in our Nation.

"WHITE PRIVILEGE"

In surfing around the Internet while preparing for this responsive treatise, I came across the racialistic concept of "White Privilege". Turns out this seems to be the primary "Sujet du jour" for many Universities throughout America.

The premise of the concept is that America is predisposed to favor the "White" person and therefore discriminates against, or marginalizes, all other races.

One "white privilege" I read about was the fact that Band-Aids are for "white skin".

> "A cultural competency workshop offered at the University of North Carolina at Chapel Hill has determined that flesh colored Band-Aids are just another example of white privilege" (36)

This suggests, I suppose, that Band-Aids are not visible on, or match, all "white" skin. I checked and Band-Aids are darker than my wife's "white skin", and some I've seen are very colorful with cartoon characters. Guess some "white" people are not as privileged, when it comes to wound dressing, as "white privilege" proponents think.

According to Jennifer Holladay from her book *"White Anti-Racist Activism: A Personal Roadmap"*, the definition of what "White Skin Privilege" is:

> "White skin privilege is not something that white people necessarily do, create or enjoy on purpose. Unlike the more overt individual and institutional manifestations of racism described above, white skin privilege is

a transparent preference for whiteness that saturates our society. White skin privilege serves several functions. First, it provides white people with 'perk' that we do not earn and that people of color do not enjoy. Second, it creates real advantages for us. White people are immune to a lot of challenges. Finally, white privilege shapes the world in which we live — the way that we navigate and interact with one another and with the world." (37)

I do not see how Ms. Holladay's stereotypical racialism could be any more blatant. First she attributes an inappropriate advantage to skin color alone and implies that it is imposed just by being born with light colored skin. As usual, a racialistic mind-set most often precludes knowing the actual facts.

According to the National Center for Children Poverty, the numbers belie the existence of some "white privilege" birthright for all people with "white skin". The following facts are from a news release with the title: *Poverty by the Numbers by Race, White Children Make Up the Biggest Percentage of America's Poor.*

"A fact sheet released today by the National Center for Children in Poverty (NCCP) shows that, contrary to some common stereotypes about America's poor, at least one-third of the 13 million children living in poverty are white.

The NCCP fact sheet shows that among America's poor children, 4.2 million are white, 4 million are Latino, 3.6 million are African American, 400,000 are Asian, and 200,000 are American Indian." (38)

The concept of "White Privilege" is an academic concoction imagined by educators obviously obsessed with acute cerebral racialism. Here is how the Washington Post says it originated:

"In 1988, the professor Peggy McIntosh used the paper 'White Privilege: Unpacking the Invisible Knapsack' to describe it as a set of unearned assets that a white person in America can count on cashing in each day but to which they remain largely oblivious. The concept has been percolating in academic circles ever since and is approaching broad usage among young people on the political left." (39)

Now there are classes being taught in Universities about "oppressive white privilege":

"Students at Cal State San Marcos on Thursday hosted a 'Whiteness Forum' as part of a communications class they are enrolled in, setting up more than a dozen displays that highlighted what they contend is how white privilege has oppressed people of color in a variety of ways.

A 'white beauty standard' display stated 'we are studying the white hegemonic ideals of the beauty industry.' Another asked 'who does whiteness say that you are,' noting 'whiteness studies' is defined as 'the study of the system of white dominion in our society with a focus on ideologies of white supremacy as collective, rather than white individuals'." (40)

(Fact: Miss USA 2016 is Deshauna Barber from Washington, D.C., who is beautiful, super intelligent and an Army Reserve Officer, but wait, there's more...she is what a racialist would call "Black"! How was it possible for her to win against such an oppressive "white beauty standard"?)

At the University of Wisconsin Madison a student will be able to take a class teaching "The Problem of Whiteness". I'm not sure if "Whiteness" can be a major there.

> *"A class to be taught next semester at the University of Wisconsin Madison called 'The Problem of Whiteness' aims to 'understand how whiteness is socially constructed and experienced in order to help dismantle white supremacy,' the course description states.*
>
> *'Whites rarely or never questioned what it is to be white,' Assistant Professor Damon Sajnani, who will teach the course, told The College Fix in a telephone interview last week. 'So you go through life taking it for granted without ever questioning or critically interrogating It'."*
>
> *For Sajnani, one way to solve this is to offer 'The Problem of Whiteness,' an analysis of what it means to be white and how to deal with it as a 'problem'."* (41)

(Perhaps the "White Problem" can be remedied by a therapeutic period of tanning booth treatments.)

Then there is the anti-white privilege board at Appalachian State University:

> *"Appalachian State University students must walk past a 'privilege board' denouncing their white, male, able-bodied, Christian, or cisgender privilege any time they enter the Student Union.*

The bulletin board is located in Plemmons Student Union (PSU), which the school calls 'the centerpiece of the Appalachian campus,' and was apparently put up by a student group last semester, but has been allowed to remain in place to date." (42)

(Perhaps the Appalachian student group are taking a course in Mind Control and are just working on a class project.)

These are just a sample to the racialistic madness that is over taking our Nation's Universities. It reminds me of a movie I saw years ago where the patients took over the insane asylum. In this circumstance it seems that the idiots are now part of the faculty. Now we are paying the exorbitant tuitions to teach people that it is wrong and unfair to have light skin.

Is it possible that some of our University educators do not realize the vast diversity of so called "White Skinned People"? Do they not understand the genetic intermingling of ancestry? Do they think there is a standard "White" economic and intellectual status? Do they really think that there is a pure, unadulterated race of "White" people that all share the same geological, environmental and biological origin? Are they really this ignorant?

Unfortunately, the answer is conclusive. I will not fall into the trap of stereotyping the entire population of professors and educators. I will just state that any professor or educator that believes that there is a single biological and ancestral category of people that are racially "White", and think that "White Privilege" is a social issue that needs to be eradicated, then these people are imbecilic.

Dealing with the "White Problem" might go even further with some of these University educators. A Drexel University professor in Pennsylvania has a solution:

"George Ciccariello-Maher, a white assistant professor of history and politics at the Philadelphia University, posted 'All I Want for Christmas is White Genocide' on Twitter on Christmas Eve, according to media reports.

He followed up on Sunday by tweeting, 'To clarify: when the whites were massacred during the Haitian revolution, that was a good thing indeed.'" (43)

The mistake all these obsessed "White Privilege" adherents are making is that they do not understand, that what causes what they perceive as "Privilege", is actually "Achievement".

WHITE ACHIEVEMENT

Any advantage or achievement an individual person has, regardless of skin color, has a history and cause. It does not just pop out of thin air or just infuse the skin with whiteness and privilege. There is a reason why someone has a situation or position of excellence. Most often it is earned, sometimes if is inherited, it might be simply good fortune like winning the lottery.

All this has to be put into the context of history. There is a simple way to determine why one person or persons have an advantage over another person or persons. It begins with a simple but profound question. The question is "Why".

The answer will not be "because they are white, or black, or brown, or red, or orange". The answer will likely be complex and unique.

Once again, I have to point out something that is not currently politically correct. It is however factual. When the time comes that we cannot point to actual cause and facts, then good sense has been abandoned.

One of the few stories about my native ancestry told to me by my Dad is appropriate here. He said it is the reason our Clan refused to go West with the Tribe and migrated to the Blue Ridge Mountains. He said that an elder of our Clan had been taken to Philadelphia by a missionary. When the elder returned he was overwhelmed with what he had seen and experienced. He said the land of the Europeans was "like another world". He spoke of the amazing wonders and said that we should learn the ways of the Europeans and live in that world. He stressed that we could not defeat them in a battle and that a struggle with them was futile.

This is exactly what my ancestors did. My band ended up working for a farm family near Hillsville Virginia and took their

European last name and fully assimilated into the "wondrous new world".

My ancestors were primitive and tribal. They contributed to the world, perhaps, an improved bow and arrow, some remarkable feathered head dress, and perhaps the most sublime relationship with Mother Earth ever experienced...but little more.

This was the same situation with other rather primitive peoples who arrived in the early American Colonies.

When the Africans arrived in America, they were very much like my ancestors, and they entered a new world of a very different orientation and civilization. They entered a world of absolute "White Privilege" or rather "White Achievement".

Admittedly, the Europeans depreciated the Africans in the same way they looked down on my ancestors. They did not want to associate with them socially and had nothing in common with them culturally.

Residue of this existed for Africans after the Civil War and continues in a minor way until this day. For many of my ancestors, however, the struggle to cope has been lost...they are isolated in pitiful limbo on reservations trying to come to terms with the annihilation of identity, culture and ambition.

The Africans have fared far better. Rather than put them in concentration camps, the Nation fought a war to emancipate them. Efforts have been made to educate them and give them support in assimilation. Civil Rights Legislation was implemented on their behalf. A program of "Affirmative Action" have given them an advantage over "White" Americans in educational institutions, government employment and corporate enterprises. They have even been given a "Protected Status" as citizens.

Yet I see no indication of appreciation.

The Africans still complain and feed on "White Guilt", and racial extortion, for slavery, but even they have no sympathy for the "Savage pre-American Native People" now exiled to rugged lands no one wanted.

Of course, it does not help the Africans when mainstream America see them running through the streets like a primitive unruly mob raiding businesses and destroying property. When there is a perceived injustice many turn out in indignation, yet even when the injustice is proved false, there is loud and telling silence from the lawless raging horde or the leaders of the "Black" tribe, or to be more politically correct, the "Black Community". Even some of their Rap music is an insult to the social order. I have even heard some accuse other "Blacks", in a derogatory manner, of trying to be "White".

Let me interject here on behalf of my "Indian" distant relatives out there under the watchful care of the government "Indian Affairs" people, please help them be "White". Please reach out to them and help them assimilate as citizens. Please give them some "Affirmative Action" and "Protected Status" to help the remnants of these once proud people recover from the cultural genocide imposed on them. Bring them back from the "Wilderness" and let them reach the "Promise Land". If given encouragement and a chance they will take "Second Class" citizenry with great appreciation.

(Oops! My Indian half-breed indignation is showing…so back to the point of this commentary)

I would prefer the following to point out generic "Human Achievements". I would prefer to think of the "Human Race" rather than "Blacks", "White", "Latinos", and "Asians", etc.

I would prefer it if the members of the human race were considered individuals rather than the tribe or aggregate. However, I have to use the racialist vernacular to deal with the racialistic mind-set.

"White People" and Western Civilization have earned privilege and advantage because:

- They gave the world the concept of Democracy.
- They gave the world the concept of Individual Liberty.
- They gave the world the concept of Money.
- They gave the world the concept of Economic Systems.
- They gave the world Electricity.
- They gave the world the concept of paved roads.
- They gave the world Automobiles.
- They gave the world Airplanes.
- They gave the world Radio.
- They gave the world Television.
- They gave the world Cell Phones.
- They gave the world Computers.
- They gave the world most of the cures for disease.
- They gave the world the concept of Universities.
- They gave the world classical music.
- They gave the world Opera (Sorry!).
- In fact, they gave the world most of the technology we enjoy today.
- And yes, they gave the world the Atomic and Hydrogen Bomb.

…But wait, I guess the latter may well make the other null and void …Nevermind.

CULTURAL ADVANTAGE

Nicole, even though there is now an academic movement to defame the descendants of the benefactors of Western Civilization, you should not be deceived. Consider the contribution Western Culture has made to humanity. Those that would undermine rather than appreciate the beneficence would never give up what has been bequeathed to them. They may disparage and discredit the contributors but they would not be willing to surrender the contributions.

The advantage you do have is being from a lineage reaching back about 2400 years that has been influenced by Western Civilization. Western Civilization is rooted in classic Greek and ancient Roman culture which advanced through time in Europe expanding scientific, technological and philosophical knowledge. Your ancestral ascendancy was an intellectual evolution that literally transformed the natural physical environment with cities, rapid transportation, business enterprises, educational institutions, hospitals, restaurants, government facilities, museums, entertainment venues, food stores, and service establishments for example.

In reality this is an achievement of humankind that expresses the potential for human progress. I am ignoring other advanced and significant civilizations since they are not relevant here.

With the development of architectural, engineering, scientific and manufacturing abilities in Western Culture, progress seems to be limited only by their imagination and physical dexterity. Where primitive native people were dominated by the natural environment, the citizens of Western Culture were beginning to dominate, in some ways, their environment. Where the native people were subject to the climate, people in the Western world were beginning to reside in buildings with controlled temperature, perhaps, not even knowing the weather outside.

In many ways this is an extraordinary advantage that, in the view of some, would be privilege.

I feel that it can be reasonably argued, however, that the quality of life, the enjoyment of life, and the emotional satisfaction of living can be as good, or even better, for a group of people living, say, in the Amazon jungle in the most pristine primitive environment. These people may have a more intimate relationship with nature and their families than we can even imagine. Realizing that life is a mental translation of the physical, then they may live in a state of bliss impossible in the hustle bustle of the modern world.

But the point is, in America today, many of us strive to obtain the most social, educational, and economic achievement possible. Most want to have the best spouse, live in the best dwelling, have the best job, earn the best salary and have the best social status available. This sometimes results in frustration and envy that spawns resentment and animosity. Rather than appreciate and enjoy what they do have, they distress over what they do not have. They mentally choose dissatisfaction over happiness.

So Nicole, you have the benefit of over 2400 years of Western culture that has been passed on to you in advancement. I see an example of this in the fact that I sometimes have to ask you about using my internet applications and devices.

However, this advancement would be a detriment, and of no value to you, should you find yourself among the Amazon tribe mentioned prior. There, they would have the benefit of lineage and accumulated knowledge and would have the advantage, and perhaps, appear privileged to you in that environment.

For the people called "Black" in America today, they have perhaps 400 years of assimilated Western culturalization. They have made remarkable achievements and are actually no less enculturated than yourself. One way to measure their enculturation is to consider how different they are today from the African forebears that arrived on the American shores in the 1600s.

Perhaps even a better comparison would be to compare their culture today with that of Africans living in the back jungles of Africa now. While Western Culture has either contaminated or benefited many of the Africans today, depending on your point of view, the more primitive Africans living in tribal conditions today in the jungle are more similar to the African culture brought to America by the first "Black" people. The "Black" people in America today hardly seem to be of the same culture as the primitive "Black" people in rural Africa today. In this comparison they obviously are far more influenced by Western Culture ("White") than African Culture ("Black").

It is important to keep in mind, however, that what we call advanced civilization is a matter of question. Modern civilization in America is not better than the current civilization of people in tribal Africa or tribal Brazil. THEY ARE ONLY DIFFERENT.

To take a note from social engineering, humans today on our planet are diverse, and diversity is "essential and ideal".

One is not actually smarter than the other, rather one is more adapted to one environment and culture than the other. Both would have difficulty even surviving in the others' environment if suddenly transported. It is a matter of birth and circumstance. Both might feel they are better off and superior where they are... and both might be right.

Imagine waking up in a place where your cell phone would not work, and where you had to chase down your breakfast, kill it, butcher it and cook it over an open fire. Likely the primitives would be amused at your ridiculous uncivilized behavior.

Being "White" in many ways, as well, is insignificant. The shade of your skin is a matter of pigment. Your ancestors, while part of Western Civilization, may have individually made no single achievement that advanced the culture. They may well have been swept along with the progress as simple folk just trying to survive and "make ends meet".

You should not be prideful or shameful of your racial and cultural heritage. I hope you will begin to see yourself and other citizens as "Full Blooded Americans" firstly and foremost. I further hope you will rid your mind of the words like "Black" and "White" when referring to individual human beings. Hopefully, you will understand my feeling more after reading the following:

REHABILITATION

Nicole, as a young teacher, your grandmother taught in the first integrated school in 1971 in our city. All the students the prior year in that school were what is called "Black". This was in the early days of "integration" when the concept was perhaps "ideal". "Integration" means "an act, or instance of combining into an integral whole".

Now the students were combined racially, and she, like myself, expected racial divisions to cease, and our nation to blend into a post-racial populace. Perhaps we were naïve, but we fully expected that Americans would now begin to coalesce into a united citizenry.

With this in mind, she started out to teach the kinship of humanity and the mutual nature we share as people.

She told me that part of her lesson included a demonstration to challenge the concept of people being "Black" or "White". She held up a black sheet of paper and a white sheet of paper. She then asked if anyone in the room was the exact color of the black or white sheet of paper. She asked that a person with totally "Black" or totally "White" skin to raise their hands. No one responded. There was some muted laughter as the children realized that none of them met the skin color criteria of either. Suddenly they were the same, in that none of them were "Black" and none of them were "White". They all had skin, and in that moment, there was no difference other than shade, and none of them were the exact same shade. Again, they were all the same in all being different.

Her intention was to dispel the concept that people were different based on skin color. She went on to point out the superficiality of skin color, and the fact that we are all the same biologically. Her point was that the racial designation of "Black" and "White" was not valid and the division it implied was false.

This was the goal and intention of "Integration". It was to bring America together as a single, united people.

What happened? Where did we fail? How was the ideal subverted?

This might be a worthwhile academic research project, but it will serve no purpose now. We need to move forward by looking back.

It is time to hold up the "Black" and "White" sheets of paper again and demonstrate the absurdity and detrimental effect of causing people to think of themselves or others as being "Black" and "White".

The words "Black" and "White", or any racialistic color designation, is actually as offensive as any other racial slur. We need to assign it to the same usage we now use as the "N" word. It should now be the "B" word or the "W" word. These words are each racist, derogatory and divisive and have caused great harm to the citizens of our nation.

So how do we deal with this debilitating racialistic affliction?

It is actually quite simple. We stop using racist designations associated with skin color. In fact, how about ceasing to use racial designations for all citizens.

We might have one box to check on all forms requesting race: [ ] Citizen (It will remind us that we are all the same.).

We should stop calling people by skin pigmentation using "Black", "White" or whatever. We should stop stereotyping people by racialistic grouping. This way, perhaps, we can cleanse our minds of racialistic words and terms. Perhaps we can stop thinking and speaking racially.

If there is a situation where race designation is essential, then a DNA test should be required. In actuality, this is the only accurate and valid way to designate race. In fact, this should be the only way to legally assign race. Skin color is hardly an accurate race determinate. Should the government or education institution discriminate based on race, then a citizen might be denied their civil rights if one individual is favored over another based on skin pigmentation or self-defined racial identity. A DNA test is the only valid way to make a racial determination. For people that are mixed racially, they will just have to accept that they are "humans of indeterminate race" or just "American".

It's time that we demand total "Integration" for all citizens and institutions and achieve the ideal.

THE ALTERNATIVE

So what if we fail? What if we cannot overcome the racial affliction that is personified by the pervasive "Black" and "White" mentality of so many in our Nation? The prognosis is not good.

Likely, we will continue to "disintegrate". The definition of the word "disintegrate" is: "to separate into parts, or lose intactness or solidness, break up, deteriorate". This may well be terminal for the social order.

I look at the violent videos showing the racial hatred. I read about the increasing racial militancy. These attitudes and emotions seem to be deeply ingrained in the national disposition. It may well be too late to avert the impending upheaval. The issues may only be resolved by civil confrontation.

While there still exists a "mainstream" populace of individuals that simply see themselves as American Citizens, the dynamic is toward racial grouping in opposition to one another. Should the trend continue and the "mainstream Americans" be forced to subscribe to a specific racial identity in a state of racial conflict, then we will succumb to the same social forces that create strife and calamity among people in other parts of the world.

We only have to look at the hostility between Sunni and Shi's Muslims of today to have some indication of what America will be like when the traditional "Melting Pot" of American citizens turns fully into a cauldron of social antagonism and conflict. While of the same Islamic religion with the same deity, a relatively minor difference between Muslims has escalated into decades of bloodshed and carnage.

Should racial hostility in our Nation erupt into a violent physical clash, then the worst among us will have prevailed. The innocent will be included in the fray just because of the color of their skin.

While the civil upheaval may be limited in scope, the casualties will be appalling. The resulting social and civil schism will be difficult to overcome and devastating to our country.

Not only will we disintegrate from within as a Nation, we will be unable to stand united in defense from external forces.

ARMED AND LOADED

For the average American, the idea of a violent civil conflict erupting in our Nation is inconceivable. Things like this happen in other countries, but not here.

So what would be the indications to warn of such a violent conflict? Are there any indications that would warn of such an impending violent encounter?

Here are some factors to consider:

"13 American Gangs That Are Keeping the FBI Up at Night

More than 1.4 million Americans are wearing the colors of more than 33,000 gangs across the country, according to a report by the Federal Bureau of Investigation.

Based on evidence from federal, state, local, and tribal law enforcement, the FBI says gangs commit 48% of violent crime, and are only becoming more dangerous. Some even source weapons from the military." (44)

"White supremacists sign up for military to train for race war — with little pushback from Pentagon

"According to the FBI, there are hundreds of white supremacists in the US army or in the veteran community. Some analysts even estimate the number is in the thousands. In America, 203 white supremacist "extremist cases" investigated by the Bureau from 2001 to 2008 involved veterans. The problem hasn't gone away. Neo-Nazi veteran Wade Michael Page attacked six worshippers at the Sikh Temple in Oak Creek, Wisconsin, in 2012.

Charles Wilson, spokesman for the National Socialist Movement, one of the top neo-Nazi groups in America, was frank about his attempts to populate the US armed forces with extremists: "We do encourage [our members] to sign up for the military. We can use the training to secure the resistance to our government. Every one of them takes a pact of secrecy ... Our military doesn't agree with our political beliefs, they are not supposed to be in the military, but they're there, in ever greater numbers." He claimed to have 190 members serving.

Wilson's claims can't simply be dismissed as empty boasting. In a 2006 report, the National Gang Intelligence Center, which operates under the DOJ and integrates gang intelligence across agencies, noted: "various white supremacist groups have been documented on military installations both domestically and internationally." Neo-Nazis "stretch across all branches of service, they are linking up across the branches once they're inside, and they are hard-core," Department of Defense gang detective Scott Barfield told the Southern Poverty Law Center." (45)

Almost Every State has a civilian Militia. The following is from a listing of every State Militias with each giving an introductory description of the organization. This is an example from Illinois:

"Are you concerned about the safety, security or future of the United States of America or even just Illinois State? You may be the type of person that is aware of the serious threats to our American way of life, our freedoms, and even our lives. In the event of martial law, civil unrest or *many other declared emergencies, whether manufactured or not, the militia is the response to secure the safety and prosperity of the people, because we are the people. In the event of a threat to America or the state, the Illinois Sons of Liberty will stand to protect our own." (46)*

"Pew Research Poll Shows Sharp Increase in Gun Ownership

A national survey conducted by Pew Research Center from August 9-16 discovered at least 44% of American homes now have guns compared to 51% without.

The survey also showed an increase of the public perception that gun ownership does more to protect people from becoming victims of crime. 58% of those polled said they believe owning a gun makes people safer compared with 37% who believe owning a gun puts people's safety at risk." (47)

The violent civil conflict would not be a typical military encounter where the opposing sides gather to have a battle. Likely the conflict would be sparked by a series of events where people from one racial group targeted another racial group in random assaults over time. This might eventually trigger a retaliatory response from people identifying with the racial group under attack. From here the conflict would escalate in continuing series of retaliatory assaults drawing an increasing number of racial agents into the fray.

Similar to a blood feud, revenge would continue to intensify the hostility creating a level of pervasive racial hatred that would make reconciliation almost impossible for the populace.

Eventually the government, military and law enforcement, likely under Martial Law, would regain some order, however, the racial divide would become a chasm of subdued hostility simmering under the surface.

Our best action would be to avert the disaster.

A Solution

The purpose of this commentary, as started, is to contribute to a possible public discourse. Rather than a prophecy, my hope and intention is to use these words to help alter the course of events and intercede while there is still time to address the social issues dividing us.

It will take a national initiative no less challenging than going to the moon. It will be up to the educators and educational institutions to change the racialistic mind-sets to civil harmony and good will.

We cannot solve this major problem with blame and antagonism toward others. We must all be introspect and challenge our own preconceptions and bias. We cannot solve the problem by pointing to others, we must all rethink our own notions and prejudices.

We must cease to declare others guilty without real individual cause, and face, perhaps, our own personal cause and contributions to our situation. We must also look on the history of America from a different perspective...one of respect and appreciation. Our unity must begin historically when our ancestors first came to the shores in Colonial America and began the struggle together in founding the new nation.

Rather than sowing the seeds of division, we need to look at our mutual experience in overcoming the challenges and appreciate what we did for each other in achieving the nation we share today. It is time that we, the people, begin to share amity and brotherly love for one another as proud citizens of our wonderful Nation.

We must begin to see ourselves as individuals not as racial groups. We must abandon Racialism and embrace Individualism.

We must cease to measure ourselves by comparison to others, and stand in self-reliance and appreciation for existing in a nation of opportunity for the individual.

Our nation gives us the equality of "life, liberty, and the pursuit of happiness". For those who have achieved a great deal more from the past through ancestry, they may well pass on to others more prosperity in the future. For those who have achieved less in the past, then they pass on less to others in the future. Equality does not mean equal inheritance, and it does not mean equal outcome in the future...it simply means government does not interfere with personal initiative and allows individual people to enjoy self-reliance and freely benefit from their enterprise and individual ability.

There are no guarantees. As in a race, some run faster than others. However, when jealousy, resentment and envy are abandoned, people with very different situations can enjoy fully their individual accomplishments unrestricted by government.

Equality, in some ways begins at the starting line going back to the beginning of linage. Some have to struggle to catch up because of the disadvantage of the circumstance at their birth. Some are handed accelerated advantage at birth. Some have to overcome injustice, some physical or mental difficulties. Equality is not being the same. The Creator does not make us all exactly the same. We have to take the circumstance of fate and go forward from there and pass on our individual achievement to our descendants. That is the nature of life.

And yet, being an American Citizen is in many ways an advantage over many people of other Nations in the World. This is what makes us really equal to each other. We are American Citizens with all the benefits that are available to us as individuals. For a child born with a birth defect, this does not mean the child will have the exact equal opportunity as all other Citizens born that day. What it likely means is that, based on the child's circumstance, they may well receive the best medical care and rehabilitation opportunity available elsewhere in the world.

If the disadvantaged child concentrates on what others in better health have, then they will spend their life with a sense of having been cheated and mistreated. However, if they concentrate on what they do have in life, then they may experience the full joy and achievement possible for them in life.

A child born in the back woods in Appalachia will not have the same life experience, and perhaps opportunity, available to the child born in a large city. Again, America does not mean equality of the place of birth. America means that the child born in the rural mountains has the opportunity, should they wish, to move to the city and either find success or failure. Whether they end up being a business mogul or begging for change on a street corner is an aspect of that equality and freedom.

This is what it means to be a free individual in order to make the most of their personal ability and opportunity...or not. We have to get away from focusing on what others have and appreciate what we have individually.

If we can instill the principles of individual initiative and responsibility, as well as appreciation of the benefits of personal Liberty, we can grow beyond the limitations of racism and appreciate the vistas of opportunity we have together as citizens. Rich or poor, our right to 'Life, Liberty, and the Pursuit of Happiness" is limited only by our individual capability, attitude, circumstance at birth, and perhaps luck. Our Freedom as citizens is not defined by wealth, it is defined by determining for ourselves what we seek to accomplish or achieve in life.

Before concluding, we need to address the issue of the Police:

BAD COPS

Nicole, you also said that "Police officers are racist and bad cops".

Not only is this yet another stereotypical depiction, it is obvious to me that you, fortunately, have had little personal experience dealing with the police. You are hardly capable of making a generalized assessment of the over 120,000 law enforcement officers in America in one statement.

However, you have every right to state your opinion freely. However, again, when you do so out loud, you are conversely subject to a responsive opinion.

I suspect that you have not thought this opinion through.

Regrettably, there are people in our Country (and in the World) that are extremely dangerous. They will kill, assault, and steal from other citizens without hesitation. There are a very large number of these types of people.

Thankfully, we have people that will deal with these people for us and keep them from overwhelming us with their violence.

Every day the Police people go to work knowing that they will have to spend their work hours dealing with lawless violent types of people. They know that they can be severely injured or killed during that workday. This is every day, all day, without any warning and without even any provocation.

2016 was yet another deadly year for police officers with "more than 60 law enforcement officers fatally shot this year, 20 in ambushes:

"More than 60 law enforcement officers have died in firearms-related incidents in 2016, marking a 68 percent increase since 2015, the National Law Enforcement Officers Memorial Fund reported.

The worst single attack was in July, when a black military veteran killed five white officers at a protest in Dallas — the deadliest day for American law enforcement since Sept. 11, 2001. Ten days later, a former Marine killed three Baton Rouge, La., police officers.

San Antonio Detective Benjamin Marconi was the 60th officer shot to death this year, compared with 41 in all of 2015, and the 20th to die in an ambush-style attack, compared with eight last year, Craig W. Floyd, president of the National Law Enforcement Officers Memorial Fund, said.

An ambush-style attack does not necessarily involve someone lying in wait for police officers; it's any shooting designed to catch police off guard and put them at a disadvantage, Floyd said.

'There usually is an element of surprise and concealment involved,' he said, and it's unprovoked.

Police have been killed while writing reports, like Marconi was, or eating in restaurants. They've responded to 911 calls, only to have people shoot them as they get out of their cars. And in the Dallas shooting, they were targeted by someone in a building.

'In all the cases, the officers were essentially assassinated before they had any contact with the suspect or placed that suspect in jeopardy,' said Nick Breul, the Memorial Fund's director of officer safety and wellness."
(48)

Can you imagine going to school, or perhaps a job and have to be prepared to keep someone from killing you. Perhaps, you ask a person on your job if you can help them, but have to keep in mind all the while, that that person might kill you?

This is not an exaggeration, or sensationalism. This is cold reality that the police have to live with every day. They can be killed just for being in their work uniform eating a hamburger in public. They can go on a call to stop a man from beating his wife and end up the deceased victim.

Every two weeks I pass a sign post on Highway 95 that is decorated with a wreath of flowers. The wreath is replaced often. The sign is at a spot where a highway patrolman was shot dead, in broad daylight, while making a speeding traffic stop a few years back. Likely the family of a deceased highway patrolman puts up the flowers in his memory. He was just doing his job walking up to the car when his life was taken. A man shot him as he approached. He never stood a chance. How could he have known that this was the moment of his death, yet, that is the constant threat he was living with.

Every law enforcement officer knows that their life is on the line anytime they do their job and they have all the survival institutes we all have. They do not want to die.

Perhaps there is no other job, other than a soldier in the midst of combat, that is as dangerous. Often they are in the same kill or be killed situation as a soldier on the front lines. Actually, in fact, they are on the front lines in our war to keep the criminals at bay.

It has been described as a "thin blue line" that separates we law abiding citizens from the criminals. It is referred to as "thin" because it is more fragile than many realize.

The people who hold the "thin blue barrier" to protect us are vastly outnumbered. I have seen a report that over 2.3 million criminals are in prisons in America, and of course, all the criminals have not been put away. If the criminal element were more organized, the Police would not be able to hold the line. It is remarkable, and a tribute to the effort of the police, that they are able to meet the day by day challenge and danger with the measure of success we benefit from.

Since, the support of the Police is eroding somewhat, and there are a number of people who, like you, feel they are "bad cops", there is some reason to predict that the actual "good cops" might leave the force. I understand that it is becoming much more difficult to recruit new people to join the force. This vacuum may have a number of effects, one being that really "bad" cops might take over. The other is that people will not be willing to shoulder the constant danger and criticism and we will not have the law enforcement necessary to maintain the social order.

There are already indications:

"Baltimore City's Police Union is sounding the alarm because they say the department is in crisis due to the fact that it has too few officers.

According to a new report, there are more than 100 fewer Baltimore City PD officers than last year, with the union saying this poses a safety concern as officers are being overworked.

The police union president calls the situation 'dire.'

'You get in a crisis mode like we're in right now with crime out of control and not enough uniformed officers on the street,' said Lt. Gene Ryan, president of the Baltimore City Fraternal Order of Police. 'I would say it's at a crisis point'." (48)

In an article titled *"Police Reveal Fears In National Survey"* the concern extends even for the police officers' family:

"DALLAS (CBS11) – The Pew Research Center released results from the National Police Research Platform survey of 8,000 police officers and sheriff's deputies.

'Do we feel we're targeted right now? Yes,' said a 12-year veteran of the Dallas Police Department after a question about police safety. The question was posed after the release of the national survey.

In one segment of questioning, 93 percent of polled officers surveyed said they were more concerned about their safety today than in the past.

'Yes, it's more dangerous, now you have officers watching their backs, even with your family, because the bad guys get to know you, they may see you at the mall, the movies, there's a heightened awareness,' veteran Dallas PD officer George Aranda said.

The survey also highlighted elevated concerns police have over protests nationwide against police-involved shootings of African-American men.

Seventy-five percent of those polled, said interactions with black citizens have become more tense." (49)

One way to make their point would be for the "cops" to go on strike throughout the nation for one month. They could just stay home and let nature take its course.

In such a circumstance we would very quickly be able to see who the really bad people are. It would become unsafe to go to the Mall. Going to the food store would be extremely risky. Even going out in traffic would be dangerous if not deadly.

We, the people, would then know what it feels like to wake up in the morning and realize that we could be killed on the highway going to work. In fact we would not be safe at work.

Eventually, Nicole, the bad people would likely show up one day at your home. They would intend to take anything of value you and your family might have, even food. They would likely seriously harm yourself, your Mom and Dad.

I can assure you that when the bad people showed up at your door, you would have a very different attitude toward the police, and would be glad to see them come even if they were "bad cops".

After 30 days, the survivors would have the appreciation, respect, and admiration for the police that they deserve today.

Racist Cops

Once again, I face a dilemma in responding to your statement about police being racists. Yet, I feel our Nation needs to address this issue and perhaps have a national discussion regarding this and all racial issues.

As a people, we have to end the animosity we hold for other citizens. Rather than deal with people as individuals, we form racial groupthink and blame each other for ancestral wrongs...solicit social guilt...judge the group for the transgressions of the few...expect the collective to rectify the developmental deficiencies brought about by diminished social standards...and abandon expectations of self-reliance and individual responsibility by transferring fault to others.

For this reason, I hesitate to focus on one problem when it is only a single note in a symphony of problems. It is somewhat unfair to focus on just one of so many social maladies facing us, and, I realize, will only cause a reaction of justification and resentment.

The counter rationale, however, is that we have to identify and define a problem before we can actually deal with the problem. For this reason I will comment further.

I want to point out that this is absolutely the perspective of a single person who would be considered as "White" by any superficial designation. I am only presenting the view of a single individual seeking to articulate honestly my feelings in hope of joining a wider discussion of racism in our nation.

As a "full blooded American", I deeply want our nation to heal and come together in racial and social harmony.

My opinion regarding this issue developed during a very difficult time. It began during a tragic event that transpired on February 26, 2012 in Sanford, Florida. A young "black" man named Trayvon Martin was shot and killed about 7:16 PM by a "White/Hispanic" man named George Zimmerman.

Perhaps each of us were, in some way, touched by this horrific incident. I will not try to rehash or justify the tragedy. It was reprehensive. But what struck me on hearing of the incident and watching the aftermath, was how needless the death of Trayvon was.

He appeared in photographs to be a handsome, vital young man who should be alive today. And George Zimmerman appeared, to me, to not be the type of person who would intend to take a life. Of course, I realize that I am merely projecting these opinions without having any insight into the reality.

But what struck me, and caused me to question, was that the reports said that Trayvon called his girlfriend during the buildup of the incident. I kept asking myself, if he was concerned, why did he not call the police? I have to guess that he was somewhat scared being alone and in a likely unfamiliar circumstance.

Days later in the sauna of my health club, I was speaking with a friend of African heritage, and I mentioned my question about Trayvon calling the Police for help.

He told me it was because Trayvon was likely more afraid of the police.

He went on to say that many "Black" people do not trust the police and are fearful of them. I asked why and he said that the police sometime are over aggressive and targeted them because of their being "Black".

This reminded me of something my dad taught me as a young teenager. I was born and raised in my early life in a poor, and at the times violent, area of my city. He told me that I had nothing to fear from the police if I had done nothing wrong. He said that abiding by the law was the best way to remain free to enjoy my life without concern for the police. He went on to say that should a policeman detain me, that I should be extremely cooperative. He said that they are taught to defend themselves and will not hesitate to meet any challenge with a stronger challenge. He noted that a policeman is not a judge and that I should not argue with the policeman but do what they said and understand that I would get an opportunity to state my case before a real judge with a lawyer if necessary. He stressed that policemen carry a nightstick, handcuffs and a gun for a reason, and that they would use them if I made it necessary.

I wondered if Trayvon's parents advised him in such a fashion or if he was instilled with fear and dread of the police in a manner that contributed to his death.

The police are necessary. They have to be tough and on guard to do their job.

Since then, I have noted that in most cases in the death of "black" men at the hands of police officers there was some measure of confrontation or resistance. In the context of a police involved situation, absolutely total yielding and cooperation is essential...both for the safety of the individual or individuals and for the police.

I feel certain, that had Trayvon called the police rather than his girlfriend, that he would be alive today. The police might have interrogated him aggressively regarding his being in that area, they might even have taken him to the police station. But he was innocent of a crime, and he would have been set free to live his precious life.

So are police bias in dealing with "Black" people? I have thought a lot about this and have done some soul searching regarding how I feel personally.

Here is my experience.

I see violent mobs come out in incidents when a police officer has injured or shot a "Black" person. Often the facts initially are wrong, and there is more justification for the incident than is known at the immediate time of the tragedy. I see these criminal mobs destroy private property, ransack businesses owned by innocent individuals. At times innocent people are assaulted, and an array of "community leaders" come out to be judge and jury and fan the flames of disorder. I even hear some justify the criminal acts and put the blame of others. This is not civilized behavior. Yes, police officers have to be very careful and on guard in these situations.

I know personally about the "Black" gangs that currently plague primarily other "black" people. I know how pervasive they are among "Black" youth and how they initiate their members into crime. I have a close friend that is very knowledgeable regarding the "gangsters". Yes, police officers have every reason to be fearful of members of these groups and ready to protect themselves and their lives in dealing with them.

I went to the trouble to listen to some "Rap" music and read the lyrics for this writing. I am troubled that the good people who consider themselves leaders or members of the so called "black community" do not speak out and object to some of the music. Yes, some of this music is a loud threating noise toward the police and they should be alarmed and ready to defend themselves.

I also noted for this writing the relatively high percentage of "Black" people who break the law. Just watching the local news reveals the high numbers of "dark skinned people" whose mug shots show on the screen. It becomes obvious regarding violence and robberies. Constantly seeing the number of mug shots has a subliminal effect that creates an involuntary impression of who is most dangerous in our society.

I think about the fact that the Police officers are having to deal with these situations and having to constantly apprehend these lawless individuals. The police, too, must be mentally influenced by the similarities of the perpetrators. We need only to look at the statistics to determine how the bias might be weighted. It would take an idiot not to realize the implications of the actual experience.

I have a personal experience that helps me further understand how a police officer might develop a measure of statistical bias...not that it is appropriate, but that it is inevitable for any human being having to deal with the situation regardless of their own race.

I am a walker. I go for walks often. My current walking route takes me by a small park area.

A while back near the park, I was approached by five young "black" people. I noticed that there was a seemingly well-dressed older young man, much taller, with four younger and smaller youths. I was aware of their approach but paid little attention other than to move to the side of the sidewalk.

When they were very near, the tall person said, "You better step aside old man". I was surprised. I expected them to simply pass by as so many other groups of youths have done...seeming not to even notice me. Then when just past me the larger person turned and said loudly, "Old man, you whites have lost your power". They all laughed but continued on their way.

Over the years, I have had to deal with situations when walking isolated trails, but, other than the occasional intimidating dog or shout from a passing vehicle, I had not been bothered on the street.

More recent, I was walking in the same area and noticed that two seemingly high school kids stopped about 50 feet in front of me on the sidewalk and stood on the side. They happen to be young people you would consider to be "black". I figured they were students because they each had on a backpack.

As I approached, one began to move up and down with his closed fist by his side. It seemed like a movement and pose to indicate he was going to hit me as I passed. His friend was encouraging him to walk on.

As I passed he had a silly smile on his face and was looking directly at me. His friend grew quiet as I passed. I expected him to strike at me, and I prepared myself to meet his attack. He let me pass without incident.

Up unto this point, I had never been on guard when I met people on the street. I would glance to determine if they seemed inclined to speak. I ignored them if they seemed to want to pass without visual or verbal contact, or would take on a smile if they seemed friendly.

After these incidents, I began to notice a change in my mentality when I was being approached by youth...particularly "black" youth since I have never been hardly noticed by "white" youths. I find myself on guard and somewhat concerned. I do not know what to expect and realize that I am at a disadvantage in defending myself.

This has led to my preparing to be able to defend myself. I now have the element of unexpected defense at the ready in a number of ways. My concern now is that I will be forced to protect myself even though I do not want to be harmed or harm anyone else.

I have always watched my thoughts and put down any tendency to project a presumptive attitude of prejudice toward an individual. Now I cannot control the feeling of potential threat. When in the proximity of a group of "black" youths while walking, I am acutely alert and watch for any gesture of attack. Naturally, I would not respond to a verbal assault, however, my survival instincts kick in and I am in a full defensive mode. I deplore what has happen to me and the effect it has had on my routine of walking. Fortunately, in the absence of a perceived threat, the physical and mentally invigorating pleasure of walking still remains.

This, then, is how I relate to the police officers. While the police have to be alert to threats from all people they apprehend, is there a reason for some involuntary bias when they are dealing with some particular individuals. Like me, has their personal experience caused an inappropriate tendency to react based on superficial racial characteristics? I reiterate "Inappropriate", since prejudice is unfair to the innocent individual regardless of involuntary perceptions when based on racial stereotyping.

I am not alluding to right and wrong. It is wrong for me to project a past experience on the, likely, innocent young men I pass on the street because they have skin darker than mine. I have no acceptable defense other than to say that protective and survival instincts are primal and ingrained in our psyche. It is something we have to subdue rather than consciously cause.

In considering this issue, I came across some statistics which are purported to be based on FBI statistics. If these are accurate then this is certainly a critical factor:

"From 2011 to 2013, 38.5 per cent of people arrested for murder, manslaughter, rape, robbery, and aggravated assault were black. This figure is three times higher than the 13% black population figure. When you account for the fact that black males aged 15-34, who account for around 3% of the population, are responsible for the vast majority of these crimes, the figures are even more staggering." (50)

My first reaction is "can it be possible that 13% if the population is responsible for almost 40% of the most horrendous violent crimes in the US...many being youths?"

My next reaction is, why are the "self-proclaimed" spokesman for the "black community" not speaking out in condemnation of this behavior. Why is the National Association for the Advance of Colored People not addressing this social blight within their "community"? Is overcoming this problem not essential to the advancement of "colored people". Why is this not the first priority? Is the NAACP simply shifting blame and responsibility to others? Should not the focus be on the real problem of making the individual perpetrators responsible for their actions? Is this acceptable behavior for the "Black Community"?

Even if these criminals are poor and disadvantaged, there is no reason for our civil society to have to accept this type of uncivilized behavior from any individual, regardless of racial identity. If every poor and disadvantaged person in this country behaved in this manner, our nation would be in total civil disarray. As I would tell my child, "you must stop that behavior before we do anything else. That behavior is absolutely unacceptable regardless of the excuse."

But back to the subject of "Racist Cops".

If the statistics cited here are correct, then the police might be under the same causal factors I am dealing with. I admit I am wrong, and, likely, they are wrong. However, why should I, they, or anyone have to withstand such threat of violence and social abuse without any effect?

So where is the fault? Am I guilty of racism because I now somewhat stereotype "black" youths as a threat? Would I be foolish and naïve to dismiss my experience and trust in hope that no one bothers me in the future? Is that even possible?

So I ask myself, can I ask more of the Police that are confronted with threat and violence every working day?

I admit it is a dilemma. The only answer I can offer is that people with no ill intent should understand the difficult situation the police officer is in, and should just submit to the authority and give complete cooperation and consideration. It will require trust and perhaps some undeserved humility, but it will put all the responsibility on the police officer with the justification of any mistake made by the officer. It might even help if the leadership, ministerial, and membership of the "black community" begin to stress the need for passivity and submission. The police would eventually realize the effort and would likely cohere to the new spirit of cooperation and understanding.

I wish it could be done in the remembrance of Trayvon and as a memorial to a life needlessly lost.

In Conclusion

Nicole,

As you might surmise by the length, and perhaps intensity, of this writing, the subject of Racialism is a major concern for me. I have been distressed by the issue for some time and felt frustrated that I have been unable to do anything about the problem

Then when you said to me that you "do not like white people", my frustration became determination to find some way, personally, to deal with the issue.

I suddenly realized that racialism had touched you, my granddaughter, and was in fact contaminating your mind. I frankly became angry that someone so innocent and socially naïve could be drawn into such a despicable state of mind. (I understand that you are not as innocent and naïve as I might think, however, you are not a viable candidate to start disliking people because of skin color, especially your own skin color. Only external influences could cause such an effect.)

It also struck me that Racialism had touched me in just taking my daily walk on a public street not bothering anyone. I began to realize that we cannot insulate ourselves from the effects of Racialism and that we cannot escape the impact it is having on our Nation.

For this reason, I decide that all I can do is state my thoughts about the issue, which I have done with this document. It has been an effort and taken far more of my time than expected. Now I have to attempt to disseminate this commentary as far and wide as possible. This I plan to do in seeking to publish these words.

However, as a parting message for you, Nicole, I hope you will come to understand that the underlying reality of our existence is that we are all, regardless of racial background, part of Humanity on a relatively small planet in a bewilderingly vast Universe. We are all part of the phenomena of Life on this nurturing Earth. All living things are our kin. We are all part of the cosmos and have a place alongside everything else that exists.

At the fundamental level, the Universe, you, all other people and everything else are made up of the same extremely small particles. The particles form into atoms that form into molecules that ultimately make up everything. I know you are aware of this because I remember your studying what molecules are made of.

The same atoms that made up the dinosaurs and our "cave men" ancestors are the same atoms that we are all made up of today. The atoms simply recycle through time and material objects continuously.

Ultimately, therefore, there is only one thing that is everything, interrelated and connected. Should you study Physics, specifically Quantum Physics, you will find that this is true scientifically.

Whatever all of us are is of the same thing. Science and Religion tell us that we all originated from a single source. For Science it was a tiny object that suddenly began to expand a bit over 13 billion years ago, resulting in the Universe that exists today. For Religion it was our eternal God that created all of us and everything in the Universe.

Therefore, if you believe in God, then God is the source and creator that fashions the Universe, life and all life forms into existence.

If you do not believe in God, then there must be a system of fundamental processes that randomly form into different states of being in a constant interchange of activity.

Regardless, it is absurd to use our moment of temporary being in a foolish manner, by wasting this brief occasion of life on Earth in conflict with another temporary being based on the outer covering of our skin.

In other words, don't dislike or judge people based on their skin color, enjoy your life, be good just in case, relax, and smell the roses.

(You may be familiar with my favorite song:
Row, Row, Row your boat gently down the stream,
for merrily, merrily, merrily, merrily,
life is but a dream.)

REFERENCES

. . .

1. How many words are there in English? *Merriam-Webster. com/help.* [Online] https://www.merriam-webster.com/help/faq-how-many-english-words.

2. Surluga, By Susan. "To Bring a Divided Country Together, Start With a Little Spit. *Washington Post Online.* [Online] December 24, 2016. https://www.washingtonpost.com/news/grade-point/wp/2016/12/24/to-bring-a-divided-country-together-start-with-a-little-spit/?utm_term=.7ab4d3020687.

3. Shushannah Walshe. How Little-Known MIT Professor Jonathan Gruber Shook Up Washington This Wee. *abcnews.ocm.* [Online] Nov 14, 2014. abcnews.go.com/Politics/obamacare-architect-jonathan-gruber-fire/story?id=26919286.

4. Arizona will be hit the hardest when Obamacare premiums go up next year. *CBS New York.* [Online] 2016. http://newyork.cbslocal.com/2016/10/25/arizona-obamacare-premiums/.

5. R. Halliburton, Jr. "Free Black Owners of Slaves: A Reappraisal of the Woodson Thesis. *The South Carolina Historical Magazine.* July, 1975, Vols. Vol. 76, No. 3.

6. Henry Louis Gates, Jr. "Did Black People Own Slaves?". *American Renaissance.* [Online] March 2013. www.amren.com.

7. Results from the 1850 Census. *The Civil War Home Page.* [Online] www.civil-war.net/pages/1860_census.html.

8. Bergman, Peter. "The Chronological History of the Negro in America. s.l. : Harper & Row, 1969.

9. Civil War Lesson Plan: Southern Life During the War. *The Civil War Trust.* [Online] www.civilwar.org.

10. Hoffman, Michael A. "They Were White and They Were Slaves, The Untold History of the Enslavement of Whites in America. s.l. : The Independent History and Research Co., 1992.

11. "Hidden Facts about Slavery in America. *The New Observer.* [Online] NewObserverOnline.com.

12. Johnson, Michael. "Black Masters: A Free Family of Color in the Old South. s.l. : WW Horton & Company, 1984.

13. Crow, John L. Bell and Jeffrey J. "North Carolina, The History of an American State. s.l. : Clairmont Press, 1993.

14. Barbary Slave Trade. *Wikipedia.org/.* [Online] https://en.m.wikipedia.org/wiki/Barbary_slave_trade.

15. White Slaves in America Outnumbered Black Slaves – Bet you didn't know that did you? *unifiedserenity.wordpress.com.* [Online] Information quoted from: .(Michael Hoffman, They Were White and They Were Slaves and Ulrich B. Phillips, Life and Labor in the Old South, pp. 25, 26). https://unifiedserenity.wordpress.com/2013/07/15/white-slaves-in-america-outnumbered-black-slaves-bet-you-didnt-know-that-did-yo.

16. Mitchell, Mary Niall. The Young White Faces of Slavery. *The New York Times.* [Online] January 30, 2014. nytimes.com.

17. History of Child Labor. *beta.scholastic.com.* [Online] https://beta.scholastic.com/teachers/articles/teaching-content/history-child-labor/.

18. Anthony Johnson (colonist). *Wikipedia.* [Online] https:// en.m.wikipedia.org/wiki/Anthony_Johnson_(colonist).
19. Slavery in Contemporary Africa. *Wikipedia.* [Online] en.wikipedia.org/wiki/Slavery_in_contemporary_Africa).
20. Africans Sold Their Own People as Slaves. *Abagond.* [Online] www.abagond.wordpress.com.
21. It's Time to Face the Whole Truth About the Atlantic Slave Trade. *History News Network.* [Online] August 13, 207. www historynewsnetwork.org v.
22. Individualism. *Wikipedia.* [Online] en.wikipedia.org/wiki/ Individualism.
23. Democracy. *Wikipedia.* [Online] en.wikipedia.org/wiki/ Democracy.
24. Age of Enlightenment. *Wikipedia.* [Online] en.wikipedia. org/wiki/Age_of_Enlightenm.
25. American Enlightenment. *Wikipedia.* [Online] en.m.wikipedia.org/wiki/American_Enlightenment.
26. Women in the American Revolution. *SCORE History/Social Science Project.* [Online] Carl Zitek, Sunnyslope Elementary School, Jurupa Unified School District. http://score.rims.k12. ca.us..
27. George Washington and slavery. *Wikipedia.* [Online] www.wikipedia.org/.
28. Slavery and Indentured Servants. *Law Library of Congress.* [Online] https://memory.loc.gov.
29. Abolitionism. *Wikipedia.* [Online] Wikipedia.org.
30. Death and Dying by Drew Gilpin Faust. *National Park Service.* [Online] NPS.gov.
31. Zoll:, Sophia Tareen and Rachel. Farrakhan Sees a New Opening for Black Separatist Message. *Fox News.* [Online]

http://www.foxnews.com/us/2016/12/18/farrakhan-sees-new-opening-for-black-separatist-message.html.

32. Louis Farrakhan Quites. *Brainy Quotes.* [Online] www.brainyquotes.com.

33. *INFOWARS.* [Online] Black mob viciously beats white trump voter. www.infowars.com.

34. Holly Yan, Sheena Jones and Steve Almasy,. Chicago torture video: 4 charged with hate crimes, kidnapping. *cnn.com.* [Online] January 5, 2017. http://www.cnn.com/2017/01/05/us/chicago-facebook-live-beating/index.html.

35. Taylor, Jared. New DOJ Statistics on Race and Violent Crime. *American Renaissance.* [Online] July 1, 2015. www.amren.com.

36. truthrevolt.org/news. *Flesh Colored Band-Aids are White Privilege, Says Race Survey.* [Online] March 3, 2016. http://www.truthrevolt.org/news/flesh-colored-band-aids-are-white-privilege-says-race-survey.

37. Shapiro, Ben. What is "White Privilege"? *Breitbart.* [Online] November 11, 2015. breitbart.com.

38. Poverty by the Numbers. *National Center for Children in Poverty.* [Online] http://nccp.org/media/releases/release_34.html).

39. Emba, Christine. "What is white privilege? *https://www.washingtonpost.com/blogs.*[Online]0116,2016.https://www.washingtonpost.com/blogs/post-partisan/wp/2016/01/16/white-privilege-explained/?utm_term=.78cac7ebcf1b.

40. Editor, Jennifer Kabbany - Fix. University's 'Whiteness Forum' takes 'critical look at whiteness. *www.thecollegefix.com.* [Online] http://www.thecollegefix.com/post/30248/.

41. Thomas Columbus - University of Southern California. University offers class on 'The Problem of Whiteness'. *www.*

thecollegefix.com. [Online] December 19, 2016. http://www. thecollegefix.com/post/30434/.

42. Sydney Hutchison - Louisiana Campus Correspondent. 'Privilege Board' gets prominent placement at App State. *CAMPUS REFORM.* [Online] August 16, 2016. http://www. campusreform.org/?ID=8022.

43. Ian Simpson. Pennsylvania professor under fire for 'white genocide' tweet. *Reuters.com.* [Online] December 26, 2016. http://mobile.reuters.com/article/idUSKBN14F154.

44. Eric Goldschein and Luke McKenna. 13 American Gangs That Are Keeping The FBI Up At Night. *businessinsider.com.* [Online] January 15, 2012. http://www.businessinsider.com/ dangerous-american-gangs-fbi-2011-11.

45. White supremacists sign up for military to train for race war — with little pushback from Pentagon. *www.rawstory. com.* [Online] The Guardian, June 29, 2015. http://www. rawstory.com/2015/06/white-supremacists-sign-up-for-military-to-train-for-race-war-with-little-pushback-from-pentagon/.

46. List of U.S. Militia Groups. *darkgovernment.com.* [Online] http:// www.darkgovernment.com/news/list-of-u-s-militia-groups/.

47. Jenn Jacques. Pew Research Poll Shows Sharp Increase in Gun Ownership. *bearingarms.com.* [Online] August 29, 2016. https://bearingarms.com/jenn-j/2016/08/29/pew-pew-research-poll-shows-sharp-increase-gun-ownership/.

48. More than 60 law enforcement officers fatally shot this year, 20 in ambushes, report finds. *Fox News.* [Online] December 27, 2016. http://www.foxnews.com.

49. Steve Pickett. CBSDFW.COM. *Police Reveal Fears In National Survey.* [Online] January 11, 2017. http://dfw.cbslocal. com/2017/01/11/police-reveal-fears-in-national-survey/.

50. Paul Joseph Watson. Black Crime Facts That The White Liberal Media Daren't Talk About. Police brutality targeting blacks will not subside until this becomes part of the national conversation. *infowars.com.* **[Online] May 5, 2015 5, 2105. http://www.infowars.com/black-crime-facts-that-the-white-liberal-media-darent-talk-about/.**

Made in the USA
Las Vegas, NV
26 May 2021